12 LIFE LESSONS

from

FORMULA ONE

FROM RACING TO LIVING

LIFE LESSONS

from

FORMULA ONE

JOHN HUANG

CONTENTS

ISBN 979-8-5816723-4-1 (Paperback Edition)

Cover Design by John Huang
Illustrations by Belle Huang

Published by Studio Yolk
studioyolk@gmail.com

For Belles

INSTALLATION LAP

"Okay, I love Formula One.
Let's get that statement out of the way
so that I can talk about this book."

I am a typical Formula One fan who enjoys watching the race on TV, live fed with on-screen action paired with ex-drivers' commentary, and follow the race through the eyes of the TV director's technique of editorialising the fast-paced contest by using high-angle cuts, close-ups, or reaction shots to bring you the race within a race. The perks of watching live races in the comfort of my own home are near perfect, because I know I am well-fed with excitement that is being carefully orchestrated by the TV directors accompanied by professional commentators giving me timely information on track conditions, drivers' performance, provision strategies, with the occasional live interview with team personnel during races.

Having said that, I am also a Formula One fan who enjoys going to the race weekend at the track, experiencing the first-hand vibe, the roaring engine revs as they hit maximum possible speed over the speed traps, the rubbers fighting with the tarmac before each corner, the wheel compromising with the brake that eventually gives in to lock-up[1] with smoke, the crowd cheering over a gutsy overtaking move that turns heads, a spectacular crash that ends with a standing ovation when the driver jumps out safely, keeping up with the lead car to work out the order of the pack, relying on maths and memory to count down the laps before the chequered flag is waved, the priceless live atmosphere of only a few corners of my view humanly possible, getting up close to the podium to witness the celebration with the shower of the carbon champagne.

1 Lock-up is the term used to describe a driver braking sharply and 'locking' one or more tyres whilst the others continue rotating. Tyre smoke and flat spots are common side effects.

I love them both. However, I was not born to love this adrenaline-rush spectacle sport from day one. I, like many others, well, many others that I know off at least, used to believe that Formula One racing was just about a bunch of cars running around in circles.

Eh! A common misconception by, let's just say, people of my upbringing. First, Formula One racing is not just about fast cars. Second, cars certainly do not run in circles! Allow me to demystify urban myths regarding Formula One in this book. Formula one is a sport 21 weekends a year, 24/7 in between those days. To me, it says a lot more about life than what is showcased on our TV or down at the track. There is more to it than just speedy cars, showing off masculinity, technical innovation, glamorous lifestyles, sexy grid girls (not anymore), loud engines that draw millions to follow race to race. With a closer peek, there are indeed life lessons to be gleaned from understanding and appreciating this sport, as no other sport can.

In March 2006, when my first daughter was only a few months old, I watched my first (Bahrain) Grand Prix on TV. The following week, I flew to Kuala Lumpur with an invitation from my cousin's client, experiencing my maiden Formula One Grand Prix at the Sepang International Circuit. At that time, I made a conscious decision to one day, hopefully, bring my daughter to experience the Grand Prix in action when she was old enough to comprehend. Fast forward to the year 2019. I have since attended 14 Grand Prix weekends in both Malaysia and Australia. I am the father of two daughters now, 14 and 12, and they have both attended three and four Grand Prix weekends respectively. During this interval, I have watched every single race possible without fail; some live on TV while others on replay due to time differences. I have studied the technical terminology, drivers' profiles, and each teams' rich history just to keep me in the game. I am grateful to have had opportunities to witness greatness, champions in the making, team rivalries, dramas, and legal battles, experiencing possibly one of the finest Formula One generations in its 70 years of history.

In retrospect, I have transformed from a person who knew nothing about Formula One, or any type of motor racing, to somebody who believes he could shed some light on this sport versus life lessons. By no means am I a wizard in this sport, far from it, but being an enthusiast for the past 14 years has granted me some insight into the sport that I am excited to share with you all. In a nutshell, I have grown and matured in life as Formula One has evolved from one generation to the next. Over 14 years, as I see my first daughter growing from a baby to toddler and now a teen, I find myself on the same path with my growing knowledge of Formula One. I cannot say I am a Formula One analytic, there are just too many details to learn, but I feel like I have to show all the time I have invested in this sport since 2006. Hence, the birth of this book. My aim is to illustrate, to recollect fond memories and recall experiences.

This book embodies what Formula One has taught me in life so far; the on-track and off-track incidents that have taught me lessons. I hope, by the end of it, you can pick up something. Whether or not you have a liking for the sport, at least you can walk away with some knowledge of Formula One racing or, even better, some useful life lessons that can turn your world around. At the very least, the next time you hear people commenting about how boring it is to watch fast cars running in circles, you can tell them otherwise. In the meantime, enjoy the book, and always drive safely.

"In racing there are always things you can learn, every single day. There is always space for improvement, and I think that applies to everything in life."
Lewis Hamilton

FORMATION LAP

"Anything happens in Grand Prix racing, and it usually does."

Where do I even begin? Formula One is a complex sport that cannot be easily summarised. If you consider yourself as an experienced motorsport fan, you are excused and I am happy for you to jump-start to the first chapter. For the rest of you, I would like to provide you with a crash course in what Formula One is, was, and will be for the future. Stand by for some jargon!

FIA[1] Formula One Championship was coined in 1950 in the United Kingdom. Formula One, by name, explains its prestige position in all categories of motorsport, recognised as the highest open-wheel auto racing. Based on a specific set of regulations and formulas, the cars and the drivers are of the highest standards in both innovation and technical prowess, thus providing an exemplary display in racing.

Governed by FIA, the championship is structured in two categories. They are known as the Drivers' World Championship (DWC) and the Constructors' World Championship (CWC). The two championships run concurrently and are based on producing and rewarding the best driver and the best constructor for each season.

Seasons, in the modern era, consist of approximately 20 scheduled races. Each race is run under the terms of Grand Prix, which originated in France, meaning grand prize; referring to the ultimate victory in the race. Grand Prix is also referred to as race weekend. The anatomy of a race weekend consists of three main track activities, starting with practice

1 Fédération Internationale de l'Automobile, abbreviated as FIA is the international governing body for official racing events.

sessions on Friday[2], qualifying session on Saturday and concluding with
the main race event on Sunday. Most track action takes place during the
afternoon, with a few exceptions[3] running under lights.

Formula One is a summer sport that kick starts its racing calendar from
March to November, covering cities across four continents. They are
scheduled into different legs for logistic and seasonal purposes. The Grand
Prix is mostly set apart in a two-week block between race weekends to
allow for logistic arrangements, with a handful of races set in back-to-back
to accommodate the jam-packed season.

In the modern setting, there are approximately 10 teams, also known
as the constructors, who will enter the competition each season. The
biggest names in Formula One teams are Ferrari, McLaren and Williams.
Together this trio has collected 33 constructors' titles. Interestingly, the last
constructors' championship that was won from the group was McLaren in
2008. Red Bulls and Mercedes, both joining the competition in 2005 and
2009 respectively, have since dominated the sport. Currently, the pit lane
is being shared with the top dogs as mentioned, together with Renault,
Racing Point, AlphaTauri, Alfa Romeo and HAAS.

Each team will contract three to five drivers but only two can enter the
race to contest the Drivers' and Constructors' Championship, based on
the First Concorde Agreement in 1981. Apart from the lead drivers, the
racing team is assembled with mechanics cum pit crew, race engineers,
strategists, managers etc. For every year, the team will need to design and
manufacture their challenger to meet the new regulations, hence the name
constructors, with limited components allowed to be purchased from third
parties. Teams invest in design and development of their car throughout
the season by testing and adding new parts or minor revision to improve
the car's performance.

2 Two 90-minute practice sessions are scheduled on Friday except for the Monaco Grand Prix
which runs them on Thursday.

3 Singapore, Abu Dhabi and Bahrain (twilight) are the three hosts currently running the race
under artificial light at night.

One component the team does not need to produce is the tyres, they are provided by the tyre supplier or tyre suppliers. The sport used to enjoy tyre wars with multiple tyre suppliers, namely Bridgestone and Michelin in the early 2000s. Currently, the competition is based on a single tyre supplier with Pirelli. Tyres are the only part of the machine that makes physical contact with the tarmac for motorsport, therefore they are one of the most critical components. The relationship between the car with the tyre and the tyre with the asphalt can differ from time, temperature and condition. The general rule of thumb is, the hotter the track temperature, the quicker or the faster the tyre can respond. The softer compound generates heat quicker, therefore is more responsive and offers quicker lap times compared to the harder compound. The trade-off is simple, soft tyres wear off quicker while harder rubber can sustain longer race distance. With the current rules stipulating tyre change as mandatory, each car must use both compounds in a race, unless wet tyres were used with rain intervention.

The host of a Grand Prix has a FIA Grade 1[4] standard circuit on which the race takes place. Tracks vary in distance, number of corners, conditioning, elevation features and more. There are two types of circuit; purpose-built racing circuits and modified street circuits; both possess unique challenges and features for the drivers and the teams. Every circuit is divided into three parts, known as sectors. This is so that the drivers, teams and TV viewers can easily identify the positions and monitor how the car and the driver are performing over one sector to the other. Over time, tracks may take minor modification to improve both safety and spectacle of the sport.

Due to the varying lap distance from track to track, the closest lap distance reaching 300km determines the total race lap. An average 5km track will translate to 50+ laps in distance, give and take. Belgian's Circuit de Spa-Francorchamps has the longest 7.004km lap distance, meaning the least laps with 44 in total. Circuit de Monaco has the shortest lap with 3.337km,

4 FIA evaluates circuit ratings by its size, facilities, safety etc to determine what type of racing event it can host. Grade 1 is the highest rating and is the prerequisite to hosting an Formula One event.

therefore multiplying into more race laps with 78. All races need to be completed within a two-hour timeframe.

Qualifying on Saturday is broken down into three shoot-out sessions. Cars finishing with the fastest time will advance to the next session and determine the final starting grid for Sunday's race. Drivers mainly communicate via radio messages during their runs on the track. They are also made aware of other means of communication by track marshals with flags. Different colours represent different track conditions and or directive messages to the drivers. For example, a blue flag is waved to cars who are about to be lapped and need to give way. Track positions are often referred to by an abbreviation such as P1 meaning position 1, P2 for position 2 and so on.

The championships are structured with point-scoring systems, with only the top 10 finishers granted championship points. The race winner will be awarded 25 points, P2 with 18, P3 with 15, then 12, 10, 8, 6, 4, 2 and 1 for the remaining top 10 race drivers. An extra point is awarded to the driver with the fastest lap time if he finishes in the top 10 race classification. The drivers' combined points will tally toward their team's constructors' championship campaign. The driver and the team finishing the season with the most points in each standing will be crowned as Drivers' World Champion and Constructors' World Champion.

In 2020, Formula One is celebrating its 70th anniversary; a milestone that has featured countless changes, updates, innovations and evolutions for both the men and the machines. Formula One has always been a pioneer in innovation, a trailblazer in the automotive industry, defying boundaries and redefining the capacity of men and machines to function together as one. This is the Formula One that I got to know.

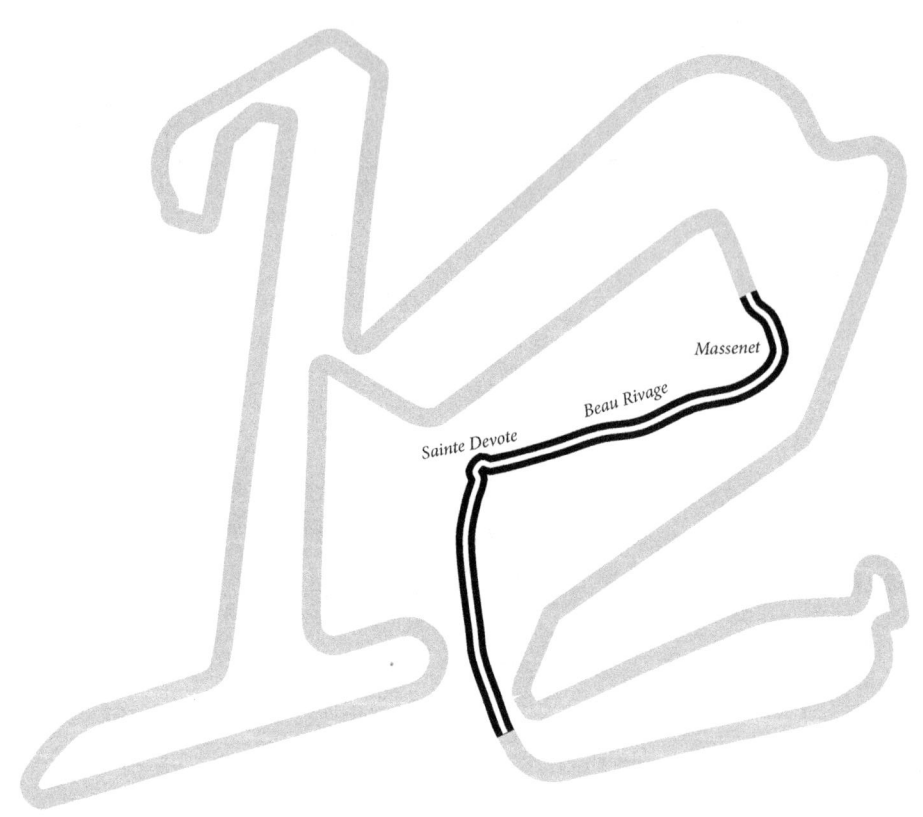

Circuit de Monaco

43.734993120665685, 7.420472541974076

RACE 1

1974 Monaco Grand Prix

78 Laps

"Heading into the Grand Hotel hairpin, second gear. Turn in hard, looking for late apex, gentle with the bar. Heading into Portier, second gear, clip the apex, light brake, stay in second, looking for a good exit. Heading through the tunnel, gradual right, up through third, fourth, fifth…"

Historical Background

Formula One is a highly competitive sport where rivalries are built against drivers and teams as much as the drivers within the team. Rivalries are great because they gain the spotlight, make a great cover story and most importantly they sell very well. We all love a good sports rivalry. It makes the game or the race more entertaining and keeps the audience on the edges of their seats. Whether it was the intra-team rivalry of the recent Hamilton-Rosberg (2013-16) Silver war to the Vettel-Webber (2009-13) Red Bull fight. Or the brief but highly entertaining Hamilton-Alonso (2007) McLaren clash to the classic Senna-Prost (1989) McLaren feud. All had proved to provide substantial TV ratings during their respective times. It is applicable to all sports and for most parts, never gets old.

All sports welcome rivalry with open arms, Formula One fans enjoy team rivalries more than anything. Reason being that beating a driver with a different car is not as significant as beating their own teammates in the same car. In fact, every Formula One driver's first goal is not to win the race but to beat his teammates. Ask any driver on the grid and we will get the same answer because this is the benchmark to measure a driver's success, ability and performance when he is competing with someone, given the identical machinery or equal technologies. This is extremely important to note for motorsport and Formula One. The driver only makes half of the athlete in this sport, the other half is the car he drives.

In a recent interview on Audiable.com, British world champion Jenson Button was thrown with a would-you-rather question: *"Would you rather be on the podium, with your teammate finishing 2nd and you are on 3rd, or would you rather finish in a lowly 7th and your teammate right behind you at 8th?"* Button, without hesitation, expressed beating his teammate is more important and rewarding.

Rush, a Hollywood production representing James Hunt and Niki Lauda's rivalry, was brought to the silver screen in 2013 by Academy award-winning director Ron Howard. This biographical film takes us back to the 1976 season when Hunt and Lauda had their fiery duels on and off the tracks. In historical context, this was not an intra-team rivalry, however, while Lauda was driving for the prancing horse, Ferrari, Hunt was with an equally competitive McLaren. In the film, the duo was depicted to hate each other from day one, because the pair was distinctively different in character. Hunt was a paddock playboy, flamboyant, charismatic, intuitive while Lauda was at the other end of the spectrum, philosophical, hard-nosed, knowledgeable and calculative. It documents their battles from the junior ranks in Formula 3 till the conclusion of the 1976 FIA Formula One season.

In one of the earlier scenes, Hunt, played by Australian actor Chris Hemsworth had an impromptu visitor Suzy Miller, played by Olivia Wilde. In the garage, Hunt lies with his hands holding a loose steering wheel in the air, his body sitting flat on the ground, eyes closed and he mumbled.

"Heading into the Grand Hotel hairpin, second gear. Turn in hard, looking for late apex[1], gentle with the bar. Heading into Portier, second gear, clip the apex, light brake, stay in second, looking for a good exit. Heading through the tunnel, gradual right, up through third, fourth, fifth…"

"Is Alexander around?" Suzy broke his concentration.

"Er, yes, he was. He went back to the house to take a call." Hunt replied.

He then jumped up and the two continued their conversation. It was not long until Suzy asked what drill he was doing lying on the floor.

"Visualisation techniques, memorising the circuit, in this case, Monaco, which is up next" Hunt explained.

Suzy looked at him and smiled.

Life Lesson #1
The Power of Visualisation

In the 70s, Formula One was only into its third decade while motor racing technology and safety are far from, let's just say innovative. Safety was rudimentary, and an obvious concern for the drivers who risked their lives

---

1 Apex is the point of the inside line around a corner at which drivers aim their cars to create a trajectory entering the corner. Hitting the apex often refers to the driver's ability to place the car in the best position in the racing line that maximises speed through the corners.

while feeling fairly helpless at the same time. It was vital for the drivers to prepare themselves before each race weekend. To do that Hunt, along with fellow drivers, relied on visualisation techniques to get acquainted with the different racing circuits. Keeping in mind that they neither had the privilege to do practice runs before the official Friday practice session, nor did they have the computer simulator that drivers of today use to practice and learn the characteristics of the track, weeks in advance prior to the race weekend. In fact, most drivers on the grid today carry out simulation work as part of their contract. Teams like McLaren have a $20 million simulation facility for their drivers and lend them out to smaller teams who cannot afford to build one themselves. In this very case, Hunt was practising for the iconic Monaco Grand Prix, a street circuit known for its narrow track and unforgiving barriers. Legendary Brazilian three-time world champion Nelson Piquet once compared driving at Monaco to *'riding a bicycle in the living room'*, proving how technically challenging it can be when a driver needs all the practise he can get.

Visualisation, also known as mental rehearsal, is a powerful tool that allows drivers to build an imprint of the track in their brains and, with enough practise, it can become operational in auto-pilot mode. The objective of the visualisation technique enables athletes like racing drivers to drive ahead of time and space. In other words, or more literally, driving with a future in mind. They are and they should always be seconds ahead of time when driving, knowing and anticipating the next corner before they can visually see it through their visors. Evidently, Renault Formula One Team uses eye-tracking technology to monitor and study their drivers' vision while they are on the simulators. It was clear when put to practice, their drivers were focusing on one corner ahead of time when they were behind the wheel. This technique will also allow them to simulate any potential battles or conditions that they need to instil in their system to react.

By the time they are in the cockpit, everything will be automatic in response to handling the car through each corner, or you can call it driving with instinct. Every action and reaction down to milliseconds will be by instinct. They need to rely on their instinct once they are behind the wheel; any hesitation costs a fraction of second on track, which is considered a light-year in the racing realm. Any hesitation is a loss. These instincts can often be the difference between winning or losing, surviving or crashing.

Part of the technique is also to train the mind to be mentally strong and believing, sometimes beyond one's capability. I can promise you, all the elite drivers who make it to the Formula One grid, are filled with big egos and are testosterone-driven with a super-strong will. To sustain and endure such a physically demanding workload for 90 minutes on a Sunday afternoon, and many more intense hours before that, they have to have both extraordinary ability and astounding mental toughness. Some would say Formula One drivers are arrogant and egoistic, and to be fair, they have to. They have to show up to work and believe in what they are doing. They have to believe they can outperform their teammates at any given time in the identical hardware, they have to believe they can beat their rivals week in week out, and they have to believe they can win the race, ultimately.

Eddie Jordan, the former owner of Jordan Racing, once said this about the six-time British world champion Lewis Hamilton, *"To be a great champion, you need raw speed, you need arrogance, you need belief and that. Now, if that breaches not a great character, so be it. Now I am not saying that about Lewis, but I think he does believe in all of those things. And is he arrogant? Absolutely. Is every Formula One driver arrogant? If they are not, they shouldn't be there."*

The Basketball Experiment
The power of the visualisation technique can be surprisingly more effective than we can imagine. An experiment was conducted by Dr Biasiotto at the University of Chicago regarding this technique. Three groups of

basketball players were tasked to shoot free throws, a close skill professional athletes should master by practising when taking place in a predictable environment. He scheduled Group A to practice shooting free throws every day for an hour in the gym for 30 days. Group B was asked to just visualize themselves making free throws, with no physical action required for the same period. For Group C, they were instructed not to practise at all during the 30-day stretch. After 30 days, the three groups were tested to assess the progress of this experiment. Group A improved substantially by 24%, a number that is fairly acceptable given the time and the duration. Group B also made progress, but with a massive 23% improvement without anyone getting their hands on the ball at all. Group C showed no improvement, which was within the prediction.

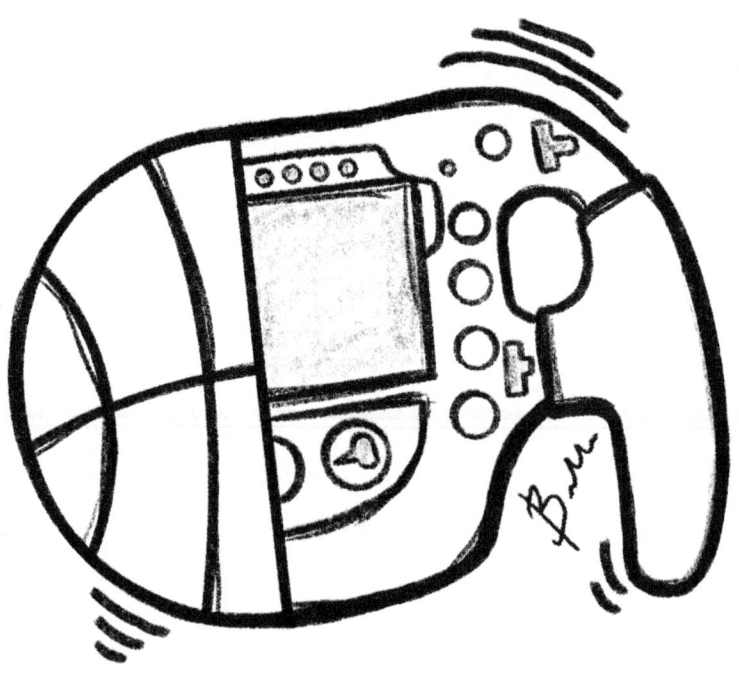

We will come back to this experiment later on.

Another example of visualisation was demonstrated through online marketing material by the Scuderia Toro Rosso Formula One Team in 2015. The team had their two race drivers doing a small exercise of visualisation on the team's YouTube channel. Max Verstappen and Carlos Sainz Jr., both Toro Rosso's contracted drivers at the time of filming, were tasked to demonstrate their visualisation through the Circuit de Barcelona-Catalunya during the Spanish Grand Prix weekend. Their goal was to see, by rehearsing their runs in their mind, who could come closer to their actual fastest lap time set on track; hence visualising lap time versus actual track time. In the 3-minute long video, both drivers had their eyes closed and both hands on their steering wheels turning and snapping on their gear shift, both feet planted firmly on the floor in an angle to allow the footwork to take over on the brake and throttle.

A very interesting observation from the video was that, looking at Sainz doing his run, his head turned in counter direction to the steering wheel whenever he was turning the car in his visualisation. He had mimicked the G-force[2] his neck was subjected to with every turn he visualised. Both drivers fully focussed with well-rehearsed and swift actions, eyes closed and no verbal cues. The video does come with commentary by both drivers to guide the audience through the circuit, turn by turn, in postproduction voice over.

And the result? Sainz was merely 2.4 seconds slower from his real fastest time on track, which he clocked a 1:24.191, while Verstappen was 2.2 seconds faster than his actual time at 1.24.527. Amazing to be just 2 seconds apart from the real-time. An assumption from this result might possibly reflect on two areas for drivers at this level. One, their mental beliefs; two, their actual skill set. We know for a fact, by the end of the

2 G-force sometimes shorten with just G of Gs, in motorsports refers to gravity force. Formula One drivers are subject to 3 to 5G of gravity force from accelerating, braking and cornering. It is also used to measure the impact of ontrack shunt or accidents.

season 2019, which is four years after the video was filmed, Verstappen had since claimed eight race wins, 30 podiums and seven fastest laps, en route to becoming the youngest Grand Prix winner in the history of Formula One. On the other hand, Sainz had 251 points, one podium next to his name and still eyeing for his maiden victory in the big league.

Though we cannot simply judge a driver's ability based on the team's marketing material, especially when both drivers took a different trajectory with their careers and moved on to different teams, fronted with different opportunities. I do wonder, perhaps it does leave us clues that one had a greater desire and belief to perform better than his true ability, hence setting a faster time via visualisation to his real-time on track. Just a thought to spare, and perhaps Sainz can prove he is championship material beyond 2021 when he is contracted to drive for Ferrari.

In life, daydreaming would probably come close to the concept of visualisation. Think about it, when we daydream, we tend to think about things or goals we wish to achieve for the sake of passing time, hence the term daydreaming. We have no real intention to fulfil whatever we daydreamed about because of lack of motivation or unclear objectives. It is more picturing the process of getting from A to B, perhaps in this case, focusing more on the destination rather than the journey. Lack of motivation and belief leads these kinds of thoughts to remain as daydreaming rather than goals to achieve.

When I was 18, in the midst of readying myself for tertiary education, I had some time to work on my application for the course of my choice. As I remember vividly in June that year, during the peak of the Melbourne winter, I would sit in the hot shower for an extended period of time, letting the steaming water soak my hair while closing my eyes and murmuring to myself *"this time next year, I will be in uni learning about design."* I would picture myself in a studio setting and working with others on my design, imagining the brief and how I would brainstorm ideas and execute the design. Little did I know, what I was doing there and then was called visualisation. Many of us, I believe, have had a similar experience, picturing ourselves in the future, far or near, with a backdrop that reflects our strongest desire at the time. In many cases, these brief momentary flashes come and go and will soon be disregarded before we know it. They happen frequently and dissipate quickly, or worse, we tend to visualise negative things that we do not want in life. Imagine the worst outcome, or worrying about something that was never going to happen.

The real difference between daydreaming and visualisation is that visualisation requires us to use our senses involving sight, sound, touch and more. In the case where Hunt was visualising his run at the streets of Monaco, he not only needed to see the track in the first person's view, he also needed to add additional elements such as the sound of the V8 engine revving and moving through each gear, the tyres bouncing harshly over the curbs, his hands firmly negotiating with no power steering, the G-force his neck and body would endure and counter through swinging the car from one direction to the next, and many more. The more elements he could add to enhance the realism of the visualisation the greater effect he would receive. The whole idea is to make our mind believe what we have just mentally rehearsed to be genuinely real. In short, the more intensity we can build our visualisation, the better the result.

"Speak as if it's already accomplished."
Mel Robbins

Make visualisation part of our day-to-day to-dos. Take baby steps to see quick results before progressing to greater complexity. Start a ritual by setting aside some time each day to practise. Find a good time when we know we can be calm and totally focussed; ideally in the morning before we

get stuck into the busyness of life. Try by just visualising our day, to begin
with. Ask ourselves questions and turn them into scenarios. How we would
want our day to be, not in general, but in great detail. How we would enjoy
our interruption-free breakfast. How we would find the fastest available
route to work. How we would spot a car park right next to the exit.
How we would nail that presentation in the boardroom. How we would
tackle all tasks in time to leave on the dot.

These are just samples, pick one or two first. Close our eyes and set the
intention: mentally say what we want to achieve as an affirmation.
Build upon the details by using our senses to add sights, sounds, smells,
tastes, touch to intensify what we visualised. If our mental image is on
breakfast, place emphasis on what is being served, how the food is being
prepared; describe the aroma, the texture, the taste on our palate, how we
are savouring it. Describe it as if we are the judges on Masterchef tasting
the dishes. Don't forget to build an image of the surroundings; what music
was being played in the background, how the lights reflected our culinary
repast and more. Remember, the more the merrier, whilst making the scene
as real as we can. The more vividly we can imagine the scene, the better
it will be recorded in our mind as a "memory". Always incorporate strong
and positive emotions. This is key; without strong emotion, the visualised
event will not seem real enough to be recorded as a memory.

Next step will be practising and repetition. Try to visualise daily until we
notice desirable changes in our behaviour, skills, confidence, etc. Once we
are more comfortable and think we can master the day-to-day stuff, step up
our game and move on to bigger goals or events, expand our expectations
and raise our bar. We will find the power of visualisation guiding our
subconscious mind to where we want to be. We have set ourselves up to be
mentally ready for all kinds of challenges we can ever imagine.

In order to realise our goals, we need to put ourselves out there and, by mentally rehearsing the outcome, our minds open up, eliminating limiting beliefs and welcoming possibilities. With that, we become more willing to explore, experiment and challenge with confidence. Because our mind is convinced we have already done it before, we can do it again. Creating that vision that we have reached the end, and accomplished our goal even before we are in any physical action creates a conflict in our subconscious mind between what we visualised versus what we currently are. Our minds are hard-wired to resolve the conflict by working to create a current reality that matches the one we have envisioned.

> *"What is now proved was once only imagined."*
> William Blake

Our brain is a funny organ. It has the power to fire up billions of neurons and spark thoughts, ideas, resolutions, memories and many more to take control of our life. In the same way, it can be easily tricked. Have you ever seen video footage of people biting on a slice of lemon and instantly felt the sour taste in your mouth? Or watched a GoPro video of people taking bungee jump and getting jelly legs? Even though we are not experiencing any of these activities physically, our brain has the power, or more like a bug in this case, to make sense of our visuals. By the same token, visualising activities or events, forces our brain to make sense of what we visualised as potential reality.

Reduce Stress
Visualisation builds a vision and sets us ready for the future. By doing so, it helps to reduce stress, as stress essentially develops from feelings of uncertainty. When we are concerned about whether we can deliver our work by the deadline, or when we are anxious about how our meeting is going to turn out, or when we are worried about the result of our medical

test, we are bound by uncertainty. Having a clear and precise vision in our heads clears out all the uncertainties in life and eliminates stress. We will be able to focus on what is more important when stress is not in the equation.

Now, back to the basketball experiment. Group A and B are considerably closely matched in terms of the result. So does that mean we should solely rely on visualisation and ditch the actual physical practice? Absolutely not! Visualisation is only half of the game, it advances ourselves by mental preparation but physical hard work is still required. The magic happens when we put the two together, to realise our true potential. Visualisation activates the creative powers of the subconscious mind, motivating it to work harder at creating solutions. We will also notice new levels of motivation and find ourselves doing things that we would normally avoid; eventually, this will lead us closer to our goals and ambitions.

Visualisation is a most powerful, yet underrated skill. It is a gateway to our future. What we visualise, we seek, and what we seek, we ultimately will receive. Formula One drivers and many other top athletes in different disciplines use visualisation to enhance not only their career performance but also their well-being in life. It is a proven skill that all of us should make full use of. Though Hunt did not leverage his visualisation at the 1975 Monaco Grand Prix, in which his car developed engine failure, the Englishman eventually benefited from his practice elsewhere. Where and when exactly? Keep reading to find out.

> *"Picturing myself on the top step of a Formula One podium, I had visualised that feeling as a kid."*
> Daniel Ricciardo

FUN FACTS ON MONACO GRAND PRIX

The Monaco Grand Prix is one of the oldest races in the Formula One calendar. While the principality is known for its rich heritage and long history, it has the shortest lap distance of all Formula One races. Formula One race length is defined as the smallest number of complete laps that exceeds 305km, but Monaco is the sole exception with a race length of only 260.5km. However, it also requires the most laps out of any circuit to complete the race, with 78 laps in total. It is the most technically demanding race and the ultimate test of driving skills; by the time the driver reaches the finish line, he will make approximately 5,000 gear changes, 1,500 more than a typical Grand Prix race. In contrast, this street circuit produces on average 15 overtakes in a race versus 50 in a purpose-built track like Shanghai International Circuit. The narrow streets require precision in race craft could not be stressed more, it is a critical component to finish the race. In 1996, the race started with 21 cars on the grid and only three cars claimed the chequered flag, resulting in the least number of finishers in Formula One history.

WATCH

1982 Monaco Grand Prix, 1988 Monaco Grand Prix, 1992 Monaco Grand Prix, 1996 Monaco Grand Prix.

DID YOU KNOW

James Hunt is the first and one of only two Formula One drivers to repeat his maiden victory at the same Grand Prix the following year (1975 and 1976 Dutch Grand Prix)? The second driver to have achieved this is Brazilian driver Felipe Massa of the Scuderia Ferrari (2006 and 2007 Turkish Grand Prix).

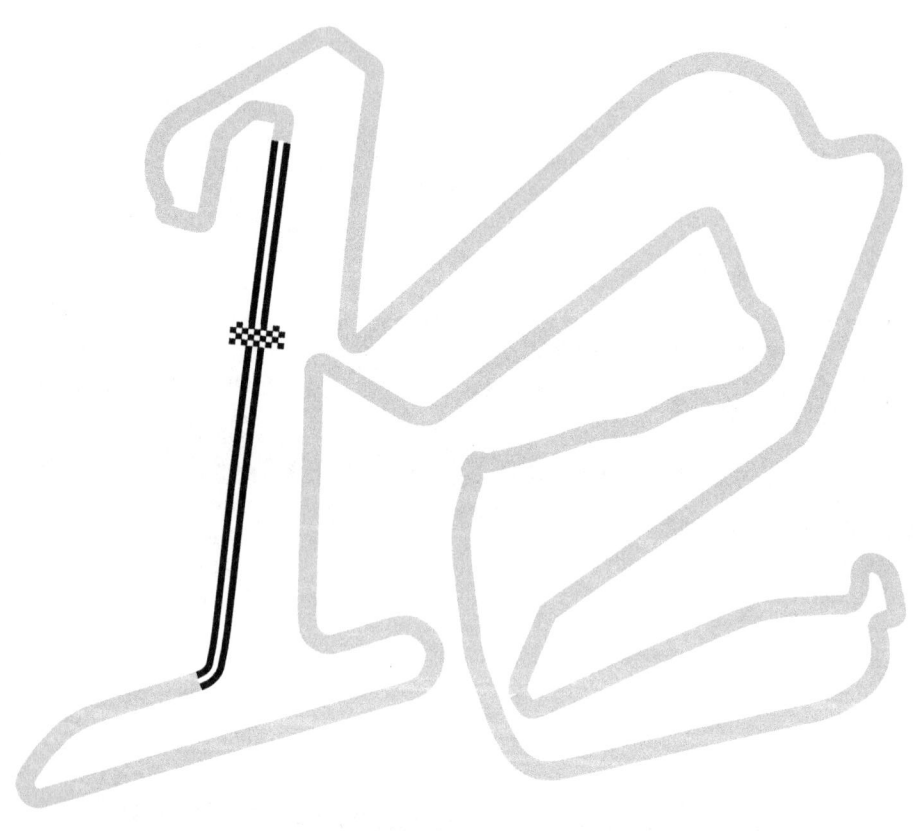

Sepang International Circuit

2.759639442277251, 101.73173458162044

RACE 2

2006 Malaysian Grand Prix

56 Laps

"Yeah, well I cannot change anything. So not really my fault but just (have) to accept it."

Maiden Experience

A day marks the beginning of a new journey, and every Formula One fan embarks on their journey at some point in time, somewhere. Mine was 2006 at the Malaysian Grand Prix. I can never forget the first time I laid eyes on Formula One monsters, with their V8 powered engines roaring, flashing past my vision in a heartbeat, one after another, like a flock of antelopes running for survival. The experience was hard to describe in words but the feeling was forever stored in my memory.

The first time I gained interest in this sport was a few months before the 2006 Malaysia stop. It was in the later stage of the 2005 season, between September and October. I started noticing a foreign, possibly Nordic name that kept appearing in the sports section of my newspaper every second Monday. The name spelt Räikkönen; that was Kimi Räikkönen, a Finnish Formula One driver for Team McLaren Mercedes. I began digging into a few of the articles, so it seemed they were race reports from the day before. The attention was on Räikkönen's title chase with Fernando Alonso, the Spanish Formula One reigning world champion. The Finn would eventually lose the championship marginally to Alonso, but it had stirred some part in me to find out what the sport, or the fuss, was all about.

I had to wait though, for a good five months as Formula One went into hibernation in winter. Drivers went on their Christmas holidays while the rest of the team continued to work on the new cars for the launch then testing and the upcoming season. Of course, I only learned this afterwards. When the new season finally swung around, it was March 2006. The opening round was scheduled at Bahrain, the first Middle Eastern country, at the time, to get the nod from Formula One. Officially known as Gulf Air Bahrain Grand Prix, 2006 was only their third year hosting the race weekend. I had little knowledge of the race weekend altogether, let alone the cars, the teams or the drivers.

I did know one name. Kimi Räikkönen, the name that was printed as a big headline several months prior in my local newspaper, so I switched on my TV on Sunday evening, 12th March to tune in to the race. I worked out a few basic rules before the race and figured Räikkönen will start from the back of the grid at P22, the last car of the lot. As it turns out, he was unable to set any qualifying time the day before due to car failure. Michael Schumacher, the legendary driver in this sport that everyone knows of was starting at P1, also known as the pole position, while Alonso, last year's champion, was starting at the second row of the grid at P4. They were the only names I knew at the time.

The race started, and that was my first Grand Prix, watched live on TV. I was very much learning the game on the fly, picking up new terms and names now and then throughout the race. I could not imagine sitting through the whole race, which was 57 laps long, but I did. The reason I did was, it was exciting to my surprise, when the driver I came to know about the sport, Kimi Räikkönen, was disposing of one car after another. Picking off cars at wills. He started last and finished the race in P3 behind eventual race winner Alonso and Schumacher. His performance was absolutely jaw-dropping. I was glued to the TV box (mind you this was in 2006) from the get-go. After the race, I turned off the TV and I knew two things I had come away with from this mesmerising experience. I fell in love with this sport and I adore Kimi Räikkönen even more.

The next thing I remember I was flying off to Kuala Lumpur for the Malaysian Grand Prix at the Sepang International Circuit just five days later. I was fortunate to be invited by my cousin's client for a treat to experience Formula One first hand. It was a kind gesture by the client for me to tag along together with a group of 12 people, none of whom I knew, except for my cousin and brother-in-law. None of it mattered as we were all there for the race, or some for the cars, or maybe for the grid girls. It was Sunday 19th March when we were admitted to the C2 Hillside area, with a view overseeing turns 9, 10, 11 and 12. The weather was hot and humid, typical of Kuala Lumpur, and we found a spot and parked ourselves among the sea of people on the hilly greens, uncovered under the scorching sun.

As we waited for the race, I had some time to flip through a RM50.00 Grand Prix record to learn a few more names and teams. I was hyped up after reading that Räikkönen had his maiden win right here at Sepang in 2003. To be frank, I did not know what to expect, as everything, and I mean everything, was alien to me. Finally, the cars started pumping out from the garage, making what I learned to be installation lap[1]. The sound of a V8 engine with more than 700 horsepower was overwhelming, to say the least. Although I was given a pair of earplugs, I never felt I needed one, and never wore them, because I was there to savour the symphony of the V8 and the tyres rubbing off the asphalt. I spotted Räikkönen's MP4-21, a distinctive livery in chrome chassis sandwiched by the front and rear wings

1 Installation lap is a lap done on arrival at a circuit, testing functions such as throttle, brakes and steering before heading back to the pits without crossing the finish line.

in bold red pigment. *'Cannot miss that for sure'*, I said to myself, indicating how the 2006 McLaren challengers were so outstanding from the rest of the grid with their metallic bodyworks glaring under the blazing sun.

Time had finally come; all 22 cars left their grids for the formation lap[2] as the prelude. The cars were weaving past me as I counted and marked Räikkönen's at P6. The rest seemed overwhelming for me to comprehend at the time. The engines were more than just loud, with 22 of them all rumbling and occasionally with gun-fire-like banging, enough to get my adrenaline pumping. I was jumpy but ready, and so were the drivers and the cars. Just a tick over 3 pm local time, I heard the crowd cheering from my far left, in the direction of the start. I had no visuals but I knew the race had begun, so I waited, I waited for our turn when the cars eventually made it to our corner. There was commotion from the whole circuit, but I was caught out because I was equipped with nothing. I realised people had headpieces to get radio commentary for the race, others had handheld devices for video coverage. I had nothing, and where I was situated, the hillside-stand considered an economical ticket zone, had no giant LED screens for live coverage.

That did not matter, I was there for the live-action. I was at least prepared to enjoy my experience, watching the fastest cars in the world blasting by. As the pack of cars approached my view, I counted the cars just as I had rehearsed. One, two, three, four...then ten, then fifteen, then twenty. I did not see the chrome car of Räikkönen's. The procession of cars finally made their way around and out of my sight; I was left to wonder, what have I missed? I asked my brother-in-law whether he saw anything different but he was very much on the same page as me. Okay, maybe I missed it somehow because the cars were fairly fast for my eyes. I had to wait for the second lap. Same cars came by, and it was a blue Renault running in clean air followed by a bunch of cars, all but one. I had confirmed Räikkönen's

---

2 Formation lap is the lap before the start of the race when the cars are driven round from the grid to form up on the grid again for the start of the race. Sometimes referred to as the warm-up lap or parade lap.

car was not in the mix. I did not know how or why and I could not wrap my head around it. Standing under the punishing sun, I was covered with perspiration and dumbfounded, with no answers. All I could do was speculate that he had some kind of accident or suffered mechanical failure, to justify the situation.

56 laps later, Giancarlo Fisichella, an Italian veteran for the French Renault team, triumphed ahead of his Spanish teammate Alonso, followed by British driver Jenson Button of Honda. For Renault, that was called a "one-two finish", when both of their cars finished first and second, claiming the maximum points for the race. As for Räikkönen, my speculation was only confirmed the next morning from the newspaper that was delivered to the door of my hotel room. Bearing in mind this was during the mid-2000s, where social media and online news was not handy, per se. Apparently he was hit from behind by Christian Klien of Red Bull Racing on lap 1 at turn 4. The Finn's race had ended prematurely, a tough and a short day at the office. His DNF[3] was caused by the sheer force of circumstances, a racing accident they called it.

"Yeah, well I cannot change anything. So not really my fault but just (have) to accept it." Räikkönen responded to the paddock reporter after his early exit.

That was my maiden Formula One experience, far from ideal I know but I could not complain. Despite much anticipation mounting for months, the lead up to the race from all the planning, travelling and getting myself ready for the live experience in Formula One racing, I was hoping to witness some repeat performance from Räikkönen. To catch a glimpse of the magic that he had shown in the previous round was my wish at the time. In reality, that wish was neither granted nor materialised. I saw none of that, nor the magic of him. I had gone out of my way to see Räikkönen race and I did not see any of it. Not one bit.

3 DNF - Did Not Finish referring to the driver failing to complete the race due to mechanical failure, on track incident or voluntarily forfeit the race.

Simply because shit happens. That was my baptism in the sport, a lesson to be remembered.

....

Life Lesson #2
Shit Happens

Shit happens. In racing terms, this often refers to an unexpected turn of events, caused by an accident on the track through no fault of the driver, also known as a racing incident. Or it can also refer to a mechanical failure, where an expected outcome was robbed before the car gave up on its own. In this race, for Räikkönen and his team, it was a case of shit happens or 'racing incident' according to the language of the team officials.

"That's racing." I have heard too many times after religiously following this sport for more than a decade, and I mean many drivers make this comment when they are struck with back luck or a series of unfortunate events during the race. Formula One is such a unique motorsport, where nothing is certain on the tarmac. No one can guarantee anyone anything until the car crosses the chequered flag. All drivers have experienced shit happens in their career, one way or another, some drivers more often than others.

Picture this, a team of a hundred staff had been working continuously for almost the entire week to perfect the machines with the ultimate setup for the race and, just four corners into the race, their driver was taken out by someone, who just so happened to be in the wrong place at the wrong time. A week's worth of hard work has been wiped out instantly. That is what I call 'shit happens'. Or imagine this, the driver and the team have worked wonders with their strategy, and everything was going according to plan on the track. The race was into the penultimate lap, and the driver was heading for the win. Suddenly the engine started making strange noises, then the driver lost power and the car came to a halt and beached on the grass just before the chequered flag. A week's worth of hard work was wiped out instantly. That again is what I call 'shit happens'.

Now google these: 2012 Belgian Grand Prix and 2017 Singapore Grand Prix, which saw many cars crash in spectacular style before turn 1 in the opening lap. While races taking place in 1991 Canadian Grand Prix and 2001 Spanish Grand Prix saw heartbreaks for lead drivers to involuntarily surrender the win on the final lap when their cars failed with mechanical issues. There are plenty more races out there with 'shit happens' scenarios. In these cases, drivers will show their anger, frustration, disappointment, you name it, just like any other normal human being. When shit does happen to them, it is not easy to be diplomatic. They will throw tantrums, have meltdowns, display aggressive behaviour, act childishly and let the frustration get the best of them. And, to be fair, spitting the dummy is not a stigma limited to Formula One drivers; Serena Williams, John McEnroe and Nick Kyrgios have all had a fair share of these on the tennis court. US sprinter Jon Drummond's meltdown was next level when he was disqualified for a false start in the 100 metres during the 2003 World Championship. The American went on a rampage, lay on the track to protest and delayed the race. In the heat of the moment, with adrenaline pumping, professional athletes, some considered prima donnas, can easily get the better of themselves, but at the end of the day, they know life goes on and they will have another crack at it in weeks to come and put their game faces back on.

"I know in racing, the bad day is going to outnumber the good days by ratio of 2 to 1, depending on what you are driving of course."

Jenson Button

Shit happens in life just as it does on the Formula One track. Although life does not guarantee anyone anything on the same terms as Formula One racing, it is never all smooth sailing from the get-go. Life indeed is a series of ups and downs; we need to embrace the good and the bad, albeit it is easy to magnify the negative and fall into the trap of focusing illusion, which I will elaborate on later. Life is full of shit if we keep seeing shit and acknowledging it; what we choose to focus on, we see. If we anticipate we are going to screw up going into a new opportunity, well guess what, most likely we will. Seeing life as full of hopes and surprises will have more chances of leading us to success. For some, it may be easier said than done. For others, it is about having that awareness and making that conscious decision, and changing the perspective that can lead them to glory. It is vital to understand both needs and find the balance in between; having too much on either side is not going to help.

> ## "See things as it is, not worse than it is."
> ### Anthony Robbins

With the help of online platforms, people whine, vent, gripe and rant more often than decades before the internet age. Cyberventing has become a thing; technology has created opportunities for many to channel their negative vibe, and it is easy to get sucked into it before you know it. People whine about life and how they wish things could be different and seek sympathy. What is worse, it is contagious if we bring that back home and infect the whole household. In my view, there are types of negative vibes that motivate you for a good cause, and then there are the other types that put you into a black hole. Always avoid the latter.

> ## "We all have shit on our shoes. We've just got to realize it so we don't track it into the house."
> ### Karl Marlantes

Why do We get so Caught Up?

In psychology, focusing illusion is a cognitive bias when we put too much attention and importance on one aspect of an event, creating an illusion and liability to make accurate justification. We tend to focus on negative events and thoughts, generating a greater but disproportionate emphasis on the wrong thing!

Here is an example of my own experience with focus illusion. While writing this book in 2020 as an indie writer, I am also running a side business to keep my head above water during the madness of the Covid invasion. My business partner and I started a food delivery service, cooking meals and delivering them to the neighbouring region. The business got off to a great start due to the lockdown situation in Melbourne and the demand was promising. We enjoyed all the positive feedback on our Facebook page until, one day, our first negative feedback rocked our boat. The customer was dissatisfied with our serving portion and had a few things to say about our pricing. I took it a bit personally; after all, our motto for the business was providing affordable meals to the community. We zeroed in on the comment and instigated all kinds of investigation and resolution seeking because of one single negative feedback, not realising it was only one negative comment out of a pool of positive feedback. We had to pull ourselves out of the focusing illusion and recognise that our business was getting more praise, and it was needless to make significant changes based on the discrepancy in value from a single source.

Focusing illusion is often tied in with the research work of renowned psychologist Daniel Kahneman, the author of "Thinking, Fast and Slow". The research paper "Does Living in California Make People Happy? A Focusing Illusion in Judgments of Life Satisfaction" by Schkade and Kahneman published in 1998, will provide more insight into this bias. In short, we allow the incident that we are thinking and focusing on becoming more important to us than it is. *"Nothing in life is as important as you think it is, while you are thinking about it"*, as Kahneman famously puts it.

One of the many reasons why it sometimes makes it difficult to accept shit happens is the way our mind works, scientifically speaking. Our brains are designed to detect patterns and problem solve. An unfortunate event that we conclude with 'shit happens' can be a random occurrence that the brain struggles to comprehend. Since the event is caused by a stroke of pure bad luck, our brain, the frontal lobe, does not connect the dots with logical thinking. We refuse to understand bad luck and position ourselves in denial, hence causing uncalled-for stress. It is a simple trap designed to test us.

When shit happens, acknowledge it and flirt with it for a moment, but never prolong it. Remind ourselves we cannot change history. Never dwell on it and put us in the funk, as funk can be deceptively deeper than we can imagine. If we realise we are in a hole, we need to stop digging because when our mind is convinced or accepts the route or the fact we are in a string of bad luck, then that is where it is going to lead us. Murphy's Law. The mind will try to make sense of things; we will begin to recognise patterns and see things against our favour. There have been a few occasions in my personal life I was in one of those funks. They set off a chain reaction where I began to interconnect a long list of problems in life - from relationship to career, or missing wallet to a car accident. It can sink our confidence and morale for a good measure.

"When nothing goes right in life and there's very little you can do, see it as a long vacation given by God. Don't force the issue and let things unfold itself. Eventually you'll get better."

Kitagawa Eriko

So, the trick is not to dwell on the bad thoughts or vibes for too long or too often. They are not going to get us anywhere; nothing more than just going on a wild goose chase. Detach ourselves from the negative beliefs that are pulling us down; take a spell, a minute or two, an hour, a day or two if need be. Remind ourselves this is only a temporary state, and it is always darkest before dawn. Walk through the tunnel and embrace life away from the darkness. Realign our values in life to combat negative situations. We could use the same principle of focusing illusion to magnify the positives as a tool to turn things around. This strategy is not something new, in fact, centuries-old. The bible suggests this in Philippians 4:8, *"Finally, brothers and sisters, whatever is true, whatever is noble, whatever is right, whatever is pure, whatever is lovely, whatever is admirable--if anything is excellent or praiseworthy--think about such things."*

5x5 Rules

Determining what to focus on and what to leave behind is imperative. 5x5 rules can come in handy for us to make decisions and move on. To simply prompt ourselves by asking this question: *"Is this problem going to matter in 5 years?"* If not, then we should move on in 5 minutes. It will at least allow us to quickly identify what is important for our future and eliminate what is not worthy of the present stress. If an issue is not going to be part of the problem in our life 5 years down the track, we need to learn to take it with a pinch of salt and march forward. No reason to linger with the "What Ifs" and "Might Have Beens". Realign our focus on what we already have; the blessings and the surroundings.

"They didn't bring us here to change the past."
TARS

Missing out on seeing Räikkönen race in 2006 was utterly disappointing for me at the time. As for Räikkönen, Malaysia's DNF was only one of many misfortunes he suffered during that year. He finished the season without any race win, and this came with an expectation after winning seven times the previous year. He went through tons of shit during 2006, with his car failing him more times than he underperformed in the car. It was a year that he wanted to put behind him sooner rather than later. So he did. He left McLaren and the cars that had constantly broken down for the past five years, and at the cost of the drivers' championships (noticing the plurals). The following year, in 2007, he clinched his world title driving for Scuderia Ferrari, and to date, he is still the last world champion driver for the Italian team. So the moral of this story goes, when life gives us shit, we have the absolute power to turn it into gold!

"What's behind you doesn't matter."
Enzo Ferrari

FUN FACTS ON MALAYSIAN GRAND PRIX

Malaysian Grand Prix was a love and hate affair for the drivers and the spectators. It was one of the most challenging races on the Formula One calendar with its hot and humid climate. With ambient temperatures around 32°C and humidity levels sometimes exceeding 80%, cockpits can hit 50°C and drivers can easily lose up to 4kg in fluid throughout the 90-minute race. Scottish driver David Coulthard likened the experience to having sex in a sauna in 2006 while driving for Red Bull Racing. It was also one of the tracks that came with a baggage of unpredictable weather, cast by monsoon storms during March and April. In 2009, the race was red-flagged and cancelled after only 20 laps due to severe weather. It was only the second time in the history of Formula One that half points were awarded due to cars not meeting the half Grand Prix distance requirement.

WATCH

1991 Canadian Grand Prix, 2001 Spanish Grand Prix, 2012 Belgian Grand Prix, 2017 Singapore Grand Prix.

DID YOU KNOW

the unluckiest racer in Formula One history is a driver by the name of Chris Amon? The New Zealander led 183 laps without winning a race in his Formula One career.

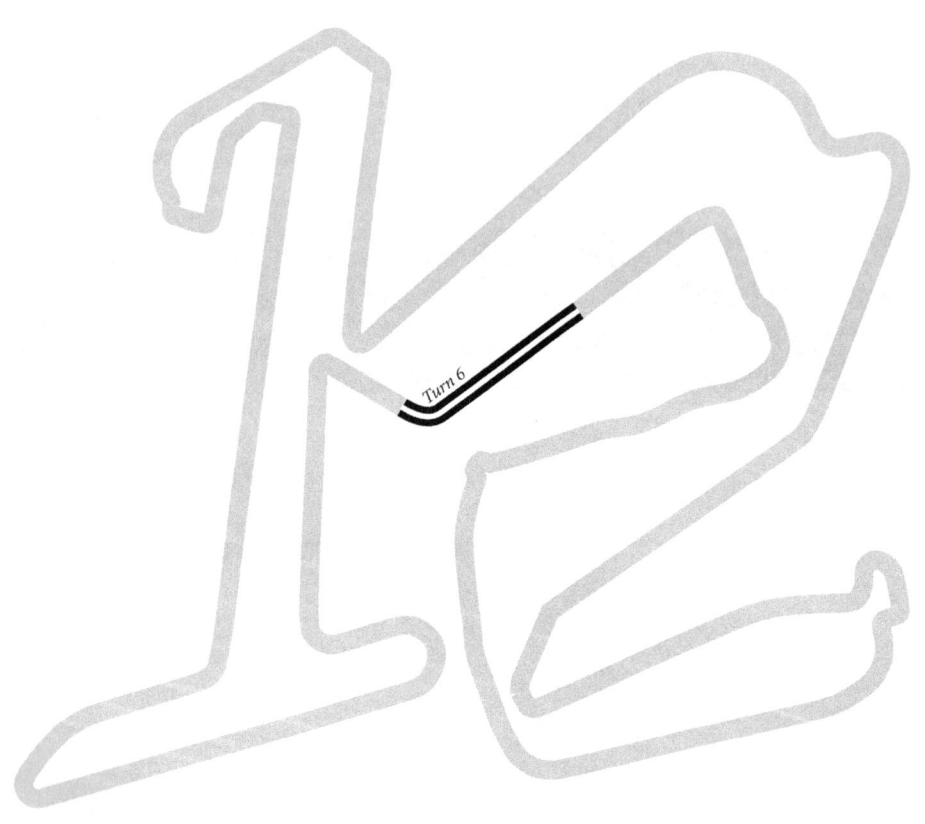

Turn 6

Istanbul Park

40.958184087485705, 29.411760731794825

RACE 3

2009 Turkish Grand Prix

58 Laps

"Take a monkey, place him into the cockpit and he is able to drive the car."

The Fairy Tale

Rules. Rules. Rules. They are written to govern for order and regulation, to create justice and protect the minority. Rules are essential for the human race in all kinds of communities and spaces. You find them in a small home made up of three family members, a business organisation with hundreds of staff or a city council of a few thousand residents to a country with millions of citizens. We are a species that are great in creating and mandating rules, and FIA and Formula One, without the shadow of a doubt, are the best in administering them, year after year. What makes Formula One such a unique sport like no other is that the rules and regulations for the sport are never the same year to year. Being the pinnacle of motorsport, the competition is responsible for the innovation of the latest technology in the automotive industry. Hence, the new rules encourage the constructors to be visionaries in building the ultimate machine mankind can master.

Equally important, the new rules each year also create new excitement for the global audience, enhancing viewers' experience with different expectations from year to year. The amount of research and development invested every year to produce cars and parts that meet a different set of rules is a costly cycle; this explains why Formula One is the most expensive sport in the world, bar none. Yes, other sports do change, update or adjust rules to their games just to keep up with time, be it technology or overall viewership. For example, the big four American professional sports leagues, NBA, NFL, NHL and MLB have all introduced new rules around call reviews to protect the competition from a misjudged call from the officials during the games. This is common practice where video playback is reviewed by game officials in times of dispute or controversial circumstances. Rules were adopted based on the maturity of the technology and practised across different sports in the last decade to help preserve the authenticity and protect the outcome of the games. Before the proliferation of technology, human error in officiating was, and still is to a lesser degree, considered part of the game.

Formula One is not resistant to changes, it embraces them. As a fan, I expect changes in rules to stir up the grid more often than not, to bring unpredictability to a new season. 2009 was a season that made a little stir to the pot of fast cars. Wait, we are in 2009 already you asked? What happened in between 2006 to 2009? Well, there were plenty of exciting races that inspired me, if not made me grin from ear to ear. Fernando Alonso became a double world champion before the great Michael Schumacher's first retirement in 2006. A handful of race wins from Kimi Räikkönen placed him in the Formula One Hall of Fame, and the squabble between Lewis Hamilton and Alonso was highly entertaining in 2007. The very same year, off-track scandal saw the spy-gate[1] between Ferrari and McLaren that gutted the British outfit to fork out all their championship points for the season and cop a hefty fine of $100 million to add insult to the injury. 2008 saw the three-way title fight that went down to the wire in Brazil; it was possibly the best season finale in decades, if not all time.

1 Spy-gate is an espionage affair between Ferrari mechanic Nigel Stepney and McLaren's chief designer Mike Coughlan, alleged in trading technical information.

They were more than a handful of races I could talk on and on about, but this book, after all, is about life lessons learned, and therefore I have to handpick those that resemble the core theme.

Okay, back to 2009, the year the cars came out of their covers looking rather unpleasant, or ugly if I want to be harsh. I guess with changes, come adjustment. The new rules required the car to be designed with wider and lower front wings, and narrower and taller rear wings. The bodywork looked less flowing, slightly longer in length and slimmer in width. This disproportionate change made the cars appear awkward to a good population of Formula One fans, including myself. Rules are rules though; they were designed and brought in to make overtaking more frequent during the race, and if the rule-makers made the right bet, I was not prepared to argue regarding the aesthetic appeal of the machines. As far as the constructors were concerned, they just wanted to build a fast, competitive and reliable car; appearance is probably the least of their concerns.

Other significant changes in rules and car specifications were the return of slick[2] tyres to replace the grooved[3] tyres; providing more grip and performance by as much as 20%. KERS, Kinetic Energy Recovery System was introduced on the voluntary ground. This was an innovation that stores kinetic energy when cars are braking and regenerate into electric power to boost the car's performance up to 80 horsepower for 6 seconds per lap. The in-season testing sessions were banned to reduce costs to minimise the impact from the global financial crisis and perhaps lessen the carbon footprint, whilst teams looked for alternative solutions to test and upgrade parts in between races.

With all that said and done, the design department from each constructor cracked their heads over the new rules for months if not years prior to

---

2 Slicks are tyres with a clean surface without groove lines, this allows the tyres to make more contact with the asphalt, resulting in more grip. Slick tyres were banned from 1998 and were reintroduced back to the competition in 2009.

3 Grooves refer to the tyres with indentation, the groove lines designed to purposely slow the overall speed of the car. They were used 1999 to 2008 before they were omitted and replaced by the slick tyres in 2009.

the new season dawning on them. Part of the success in designing a championship-winning car is whether one team can interpret the rules better than the other, finding ways to sidestep the new rules or picking up loopholes and exploiting them to their advantage. In 2009, the loophole or the hashtag keywords were "double diffuser" or "double-decker diffuser". A diffuser in a Formula One car is fitted at the rear end, acting as a device to expand air flow, improving the downforce[4] of the car when travelling at high speed. It is a critical component for the aerodynamics of a Formula One car. In short, a double-decker diffuser came with the design with extra expansion, allowing more air flow underneath the car to gain extra performance. Only three teams adopted the double diffuser design. Panasonic Toyota Racing, AT&T Williams and Brawn GP Formula 1 Team all had double diffusers fitted at the back of their cars. Notably, this was reflected in their results, with Toyota claiming three podium finishes out of the first four races. But it was not Toyota or the Williams the paddock was fussing about in the early part of 2009, it was the Brawn that was making the headlines.

Brawn's BPG001, was a beast out of the gate, it was blisteringly fast right out of the box. Taming the beast were the British superstar Jenson Button and Brazilian veteran Rubens Barrichello. Despite some scepticism from myself, the impressive time the two drivers had set during pre-season testing was considered showboating[5]. My doubts were, while most teams tend to sandbag their car before the first race, Brawn needed to do otherwise. Given the circumstances of Brawn GP's fresh start in Formula One, they needed to impress potential sponsors, hence a bit of showboating would get them a huge incentive in return. That was my initial impression at least.

According to Button though, in his book "Life to the Limit: My Autobiography", from his first ride during pre-season testing, he knew

---

4 Downforce is the aerodynamic force that is applied in a downward direction as a car travels forwards. This is harnessed to improve a car's traction and its handling through corners.

5 Showboating is a strategy employed by teams to purposely fill the car with minimum fuel and set a fast time on the timing sheet during the pre-season testing creating misleading data to secure sponsorship and funding.

they had produced a very special car. The car was a pleasure to drive according to Button. He was not wrong; the Brit took the chequered flag five times in the first six races in 2009, whilst rivals were busy dealing with elephants in their rooms, and protesting the legality of the double diffuser with FIA. Of course, it was legal, well, at least according to FIA's final ruling. The rivals had no choice but to go back to their drawing boards to introduce their versions of the double diffuser to balance the competition. Would it matter? Button already had a whopping lead over the rest of the competition before Round 7 of the Turkish Grand Prix.

The host for this event, Istanbul Park is known for its super-long, four-apex turn 8 feature, known as "Diabolica". Sixth gear and going flat out at 200kph through the corner easily produces loads and stress on both the tyres and the drivers. On Sunday 7th of June, Sebastian Vettel of the Red Bull Racing was in the box seat for the second time in seven race starts, and was ready to take on the challenge of turn 8. Championship leader Button was alongside him on P2, followed by his teammate Barrichello. Mark Webber of Red Bull and Jarno Trulli of Toyota were P4 and P5 respectively. With 58 laps ahead of them, the five lights went off, and the race got underway. It was a perfect start for Vettel as he pulled away from the pack after turn 1. Nothing was won or lost through turn 1, albeit the race was still young. For Vettel, a 20-year-old prodigy of Red Bull's young driver's program, he had a lot to prove. He was pressing hard to work his way to his maiden win with the Austrian team. His previous and only race win came a year earlier with the sister team Toro Rosso in a wet Monza race. Expectations were high on the young German, and starting from pole and seemingly running away from the rest of the field was a great showing of his determination. Perhaps a bit too much, undermining the 5 G-force from turn 8. Yes, the stressful Diabolica corner had him. Instead of letting the race come to him, Vettel pushed too hard through turn 8; there and then, the inexperienced Vettel lost it and went wide, gifting away P1 to Button. To cut to the chase, Button in return thanked the German and ran

home with his sixth victory of the season. His confidence in piloting his
BGP001 was through the roof after that dominant weekend.

Brawn GP was the Cinderella story of the Formula One paddock in 2009;
they were like the rise of the phoenix from the ashes for what they had been
through. Before they became Brawn GP, they were known as Honda Racing
F1 team, an operation owned by the Japanese motorsport giant. Honda
decided to pull out of the sport and concluded their life in the fast lane at
the end of the 2008 season. The team principal Ross Brawn along with
chief executive Nick Fry saw something in the team for 2009 and beyond.
They purchased the team themselves and ran under the new name Brawn
GP just weeks before the first pre-season testing session of the year. It was a
gamble in many people's eyes and, to cut a long story short, much to Brawn
and Fry's credit, they made it to the opening round in Melbourne. Wait,
let me rephrase it. They did not just make it to the grid, they flabbergasted
the world by snatching pole and race win in the team's maiden outing. Not
something you get to see often and it was not a fluke by any chance.

Coming back to Istanbul, Button and Brawn were easily more superior
on the day, and it did look like they were going to run away with the title
with just more than half of the season remaining. Little did he know that
the Turkish Grand Prix would be his last win with the team for the season.
What happened between Istanbul to the last race at Abu Dhabi? Nothing.
I mean literally nothing. Nothing as in, no development to their cars in
between the year because of the team's cash flow and budget. We all know
money talks in motor racing, and it costs an arm and leg to run and sustain
a Formula One team. While every other team continued the development
of their cars by bringing 5,000 new components every fortnight to the race
to improve performance, Brawn simply did not have the same luxury of
in-season upgrades. They had brought in a new front wing and had
to survive with just three chassis for the entire season. With no further
development, the car was not given the opportunity to evolve.

Formula One teams will go to great lengths in in-season development as long as the rule and funds permit. In one of the Red Bull Racing's behind the scene footage, mechanic Ole Schack was explaining how they need to build the car a week before the race and he is happy to run this with a tight schedule, provided teams have come up with new parts to help develop the car. *"If you got every single part available a week before, you have not pushed your development far enough. You know that's how this game works. If you say you already two weeks in advance and there's nothing new, you'd probably not try hard enough. So I don't mind and I don't think anybody mind having the parts late because it's been part of the way we operate, we trying to get the most, extract the most performance out of these cars. There's no good having them sitting in here being you know if they could have been four-tenths quicker during the race weekend if we have the new parts and we would rather just take it all apart and we get to the other end make sure we beat them all."*

To give a reference point on Formula One cars' in-season development, the expectation translates into the performance of the machine. The first car that breaks cover and enters the first race of the season has its fastest time as the slowest time for the car that was developed throughout the year entering the last race of the season. Evolution is part of the competition before and during the season for all Formula One cars.

Life Lesson #3

The Evolution Game

Life itself is an evolution. I am not talking about biological evolution, not the theory that we all come from fish, I am referring to the evolution of oneself. We evolve each day we wake up, physically, mentally and spiritually. We are supposed to better ourselves, each day, if not every time the earth revolves around the sun to take its course. We evolve in many forms and shapes and, since I just touched on the earth making its turn around the sun, I was referring to how we evolve through our new year resolutions; the list of goals we wish to achieve from a new beginning. Each year, we hope to become better individuals, evolving into our better selves; that is if we stick to them every time, every year.

At other times, evolution happens more naturally in the background without much of a choice, just as the FIA enforces new rules and regulations upon a new season which the teams and drivers have to adapt. The way the drivers approach the Grand Prix weekend is far different from those who competed 20 years ago; different rules with different machines come with different expectations. All for the well-being of the sport. We could easily argue that life was different 30 years ago and how we as a human race have leapt into an era that is now technology-driven. We evolve from learning, through books or life experiences; we evolve from adapting to changes in life by striving for survival.

> *"Find out what the next thing is that you can push, that you can invent, that you can be ignorant about, that you can be arrogant about, that you can fail with, and that you can be a fool with. Because in the end, that's how you grow."*
> Paula Scher

The Two-edged Sword
The fact is, the world is evolving as you read this book. We all are impelled to keep up, one way or another, for better or for worse; the two-edged sword which is the evolution game. Our lives evolve for the better when

technology continues to push in leaps and bounds. We have the world at our fingertips, with one single device in our hand, we can achieve tasks in a matter of seconds that would have taken hours if not days in the past. The convenience of information allows us to achieve more as a human being, at the same time making us more dependent on technology and anxious than ever before. The advancement of technology claims to bring people closer together; video conferences allow us to see loved ones from the other side of the world, at the same time creating gaps in the ones that are closer to us. How often do we see people on their phones in a social gathering space? That is not for you to answer or even ponder. It is rhetorical.

Google "Gif technology evolution" and you shall see a short animation clip compiling a table of items we used to see on a typical working desk in the early 90s. Items and tools include a classic Mac desktop computer, landline telephone, fax machine, alarm clock, polaroid camera, rotary address card file, newspaper, calendar, photo frame, memo board, encyclopaedia, books, desk globe and more. A lot of these items I trust millennials nowadays have not seen before. The animation started with a table full and quickly eliminated items that were obsolete through time and, by the end of that 5-second long animation, all the items had transformed into apps that either sat on the desktop of the laptop computer or the smartphone beside it.

> ### "We live in a different world than we did just 30 seconds ago."
> Sonny Weaver Jr.

That is the story of our generation; the two items that dictate our daily life in the year 2020. To say this technology evolution progresses our performance or efficiency is only half of the story. The flip side is the loss of ability to remember names, addresses, telephone numbers that we all were so good at. The ability to do mental maths with a snap of our fingers.

We become more dependent on technology and vulnerable without it. We would be more anxious if we left the house today without a smartphone than our wallet or purse. We would be lost for direction, pun intended, without Google Maps. Most importantly, we have lost the ability, or rather the opportunity, to connect to people in real life. Instead many tend to seek instant gratification through online spaces, yearning for likes, friends, followers, retweets, reposts, subscriptions and all kinds of compulsion.

While technology such as a smart device is supposed to bring convenience and productivity to our lives, I have my doubts. For instance, our attachment to emails and notifications have gotten in the way of being productive, as opposed to the days without. We are now responsible and expected to constantly check for incoming mail and, in the process, deal with spam and junk in between; checking emails first thing in the morning, sometimes even before we get out of bed. We reply to these emails while we commute in public transport, at the airport lounge waiting for our flights or during dinner with our family. While we are expected to be productive, these things has also become a distraction in our life. With technology vying for our attention, the empty slots in between our days have now been filled with all kinds of notifications, pins and interruptions, acting as more of a counterproductive activity. We can hardly focus on tasks at hand, even if they are leisure or family activities; these notifications can be quite a nuisance and distraction to our world. The expectation to be able to multitask gave away the right to give our undivided attention to the ones that deserve it. Just my thought to spare.

> *"Our sport is unique. It is man against man, machine against machine. But the machine has completely changed over time, and the world around it too."*
>
> Jean Todt

Formula One has evolved in many aspects in a similar manner. Safety has come a long way with design and materials that protects the pilots. Carbon fibre[6] introduced by McLaren in 1981, was probably the best thing since sliced bread, given how lightweight and strong it is to sustain multiple Gs during impact from a shunt. In the 2007 Canadian Grand Prix, Robert Kubica of BMW Sauber survived a horrific crash where he impacted a concrete wall at 75G while in flight at 230kph. With that comes improved viewing, where the audience can engage with a race more closely through data, information and choice of various camera angles during the race, raising our expectations. Technical data can be shared from the official websites to extend knowledge from the fans' point of view, while social media platforms have bridged the gap between fans and their favourite drivers, leveraging fandom.

For the teams, mechanics cum pit crew had to evolve their roles to cater to rule changes as well. As refueling[7] was banned after 2009, more focus and emphasis was placed on the efficiency of the tyre change during the standard pit stop; it has become more significant and crucial to conduct a flawless tyre change during the race. Prior to 2009, refuelling could take up to 8 seconds whilst the tyre change took only one-third of that time, hence refuelling could easily cover the time for the tyre change. Over the years, the record for a tyre change in pit stop has been dramatically improved from 2.4 to merely 1.82 seconds. A world record that was proudly achieved by Red Bull Racing in the 2019 Brazilian Grand Prix.

For the drivers, KERS, and later in the years, ERS[8] and DRS[9] are the technology that force the drivers to change the way they race. Arguably

---

6 Carbon fibre is a composite material made from strands of carbon and woven together into a layer of fabric, cut into shape and bake to form light but strong components.

7 Refuelling was first banned in the 80s due to safety concerns, it was reintroduced in 1994 and then banned again after 2009. Refuelling brings in a tactical aspect of the race where teams can strategise their race with the amount of fuel to put into the car during different phases of the race.

8 ERS stands for Energy Recovery Systems, it harnesses waste heat energy and waste kinetic energy. This energy is then stored and subsequently used to propel the car.

9 DRS stands for Drag Reduction System. It is a system where the driver can control adjustable rear wings to reduce drag while following a car within one second. Drivers can only activate to open up the flap at the designated DRS zones when they are behind a car. It is designed to boost overtaking.

with DRS, drivers need to be more conscious and organised with their overtaking plans of attack. Drivers are taking fewer chances nowadays, knowing where the DRS zones are, to prepare for attack or defence. In short, drivers are constantly changing the way they need to drive to adapt not only to the changes in their machines but also the revision of the rules. This part of the game has taken its toll and made the artificial overtakes less of a spectacle than in the past. In this case, the drivers and the fans both had to live with it.

> ## *"It is not always possible to be the best, but it is always possible to improve your own performance."*
> ### Sir Jackie Stewart

The constructors, namely, the designers and aerodynamicists, would push the envelope to rise to the technical challenge, trying to outfox rivals, and sometimes this meant being radical with their visions. In this way, we are able to witness some of the creative and sometimes absurd (in function) design features in Formula One cars. The X-wings pioneered by Tyrell in the 1997 season proved to be one that had many people turning their heads, or rather, shaking them. The X-wings were recycled parts that protrude vertically on each side of the car to supposedly gain an aerodynamic advantage. A few teams copied the idea but it was quickly outlawed one season later. In more recent times, McLaren invented the F-duct in the 2010 season, an air inlet device mounted on the upper monocoque[10]. It needed the driver to activate the device by moving their leg to cover the hole in the cockpit to alter the airflow and create extra performance at about 9kph faster on straight-line speed. Like any good invention, teams started copying and introducing their versions of the F-duct, with Ferrari's version requiring the driver to use their hand to cover

10 Monocoque is a French term meaning "single hull", referring to the structural shell that is built to protect the driver. Some call it a safety cell, survival cell, safety capsule.

the hole whilst driving one-handed on a straight. Yes, you read it right, driving with one hand at 300kph to gain competitive advantage. This is how Formula One teams and drivers will go to great lengths to win. This practice soon raised safety concerns and was banned by the end of the season.

*"If you're in motorsport, the formulas
are always changing, the regulations,
the tyres, the power, the type of engines,
it keeps you excited."*

Jenson Button

Generation of Monkeys

A side note on how the technology has advanced from the days of the Niki Lauda to say Sebastian Vettel's generation. A question from the floor during the Abu Dhabi Grand Prix drivers' press conference in 2014 could possibly reflect on the nature of evolution. Walter Coster from the German media asked the following question to his fellow compatriot:

"Gentlemen, a short view back to the past. 30 years ago, Niki Lauda told us 'take a monkey, place him into the cockpit and he is able to drive the car.' 30 years later, Sebastian told us 'I had to start my car like a computer, it's very complicated.' And Nico Rosberg said that during the race – I don't remember what race - he pressed the wrong button on the wheel. Question for you both: is Formula One driving today too complicated with twenty and more buttons on the wheel, are you too much under effort, under pressure? What are your wishes for the future concerning the technical programme during the race? Less buttons, more? Or less and more communication with your engineers?"

Vettel made a well thought out reply:

"I think it all depends on how the monkey grows up these days. I think it's a different generation of monkeys that Niki was talking about probably compared to monkeys we have today. Obviously there's a lot of buttons on the steering wheel, probably too many but I think for us, we grow up like that, it's a different generation. I think if you put a modern phone in Niki's hands, I'm not sure he would know what to do – sorry Niki. I think it's what you get used to. For sure, when I started, for example, in Formula One, there were a lot of procedures I had to learn, a lot of buttons I needed to know how to control etc. But it's part of cars nowadays. If you jump into a normal road car, there's also plenty of buttons but in the end the most important bit is the steering wheel, turning the car left and right and the accelerator at the bottom. I think the basics haven't changed and that's the important thing, that the sport remains as it has been many many years ago despite how many buttons you have on the steering wheel."

As unbeatable as Button's BGP001 was in Istanbul, Brawn GP could not help to progress further during the season. As much as the British outfit wanted to make hay while the sun shone, their rivals were slowly chipping away the 39 points lead Button and and his team had built up. It was evident that other teams had caught up, whether through their adaptation of the double diffuser or developing parts that gain ground on the track, tenth seconds by tenth seconds each race. For Brawn and Button, it was an overachievement, even if they failed to win either championship in 2009; nobody expected the ex-Honda team that struggled on and off the track could bounce back in such fashion. But this is Formula One's version of the Cinderella fairy tale coming to life. They maximised the aerodynamic package to the fullest capacity with the game-changing double diffuser, proving doubters, and even with a struggling second half, they had just enough in the bag to clinch both titles, giving Button and Brawn GP their first and only driver and constructor world championships.

"Change is inevitable, growth is optional."
John C. Maxwell

In an Oscar-winning speech, Matthew McConaughey from Dallas Buyers Club gave a perfect explanation of evolution:

"To my hero, that's who I chase. When I was 15 years old, a very important person in my life came to me and said 'who is your hero?' I said I don't know, I gotta think about that, give me a couple of weeks. I come back two weeks later, this person comes up and says 'who's your hero?' I said I thought about it. You know who it is, I said it's me in ten years. So I turned 25 ten years later, that same person comes to me and says 'so are you a hero?' Not even close. No no no. he said why and I said my hero is me at 35. So you see every day every week every month and every year of my life, my hero is always ten years away. I am never gonna be my hero. I am not gonna obtain that I know I'm not and that's

just fine with me cause that keeps me with somebody to keep on chasing. So to any of us. Whatever those things are, whatever it is we look up to, whatever we look forward to, and whoever we are chasing. To that I say Amen, to that I say alright alright alright. To that, I say just keep learning huh. Thank you."

We are a progressive race and therefore evolution is inevitable. It is a phenomenon that pushes the human race more than just to survive and prolong the existence of our kind. We all are part of evolution, and the world is evolving around us, as we are to them. Evolution is embraced as it produces diversity. Develop a growth mindset and avoid becoming the person who claims to have 20 years of experience in their CV when they actually mean that they have only one year of experience 20 times. Brawn GP did not only need to embrace change, they had accepted the cards they had been dealt and played the game as it was. When performance advantages such as the double diffuser are outlawed, everyone will need to find the next gain and lift their games and evolve. That is the rule for Formula One and for the world in which we live. We need to build resilience to the regulatory changes. Whilst we all are on our own evolution program, we proceed and progress through our evolution at our own pace against the world to be the best version of ourselves. Like it or not, we all have to change and grow older, if not wiser.

"You don't expect to be at the top of the mountain the day you start climbing."
Ron Dennis

FUN FACTS ON BRAWN EVOLUTION

Brawn GP is part of a rich history of various combined brands. The original constructor was known as The Tyrell Racing established in 1971. The Tyrell team enjoyed success with the help of Sir Jackie Stewart, winning three world championships for the UK based team. The team failed to keep up with the race and was acquired by British Racing Team, also known as BAR, in 1999. They entered 118 Grand Prix races between 1999 to 2005 before the team's next evolution when Japanese automobile giant Honda wanted to be part of the Formula One family as a manufacturer team. The BAR-Honda only lasted three seasons but managed to claim a race victory by Jenson Button in a wet Hungarian Grand Prix in 2006. The Honda brand was sold to Brawn for one pound on the eve of the 2009 season, becoming the Cinderella fairy tale that turned them into world champions overnight. Mercedes bought Brawn at the end of 2009 and prolonged the success that had been established by Ross Brawn and they became one of the most dominant franchises in modern Formula One, with Lewis Hamilton and Nico Rosberg winning consecutive championships from 2014 to 2019.

WATCH

2009 Australian Grand Prix, 2009 Turkish Grand Prix, 2009 Brazilian Grand Prix.

DID YOU KNOW

Ross Brawn, the mastermind behind the scene has helped his teams, Benetton Renault, Scuderia Ferrari and Brawn GP to win seven drivers' title and eight constructors' championships from 1997 to 2009? He is also the catalyst for setting the winning foundation with Mercedes F1 Team and its current domination in Formula One.

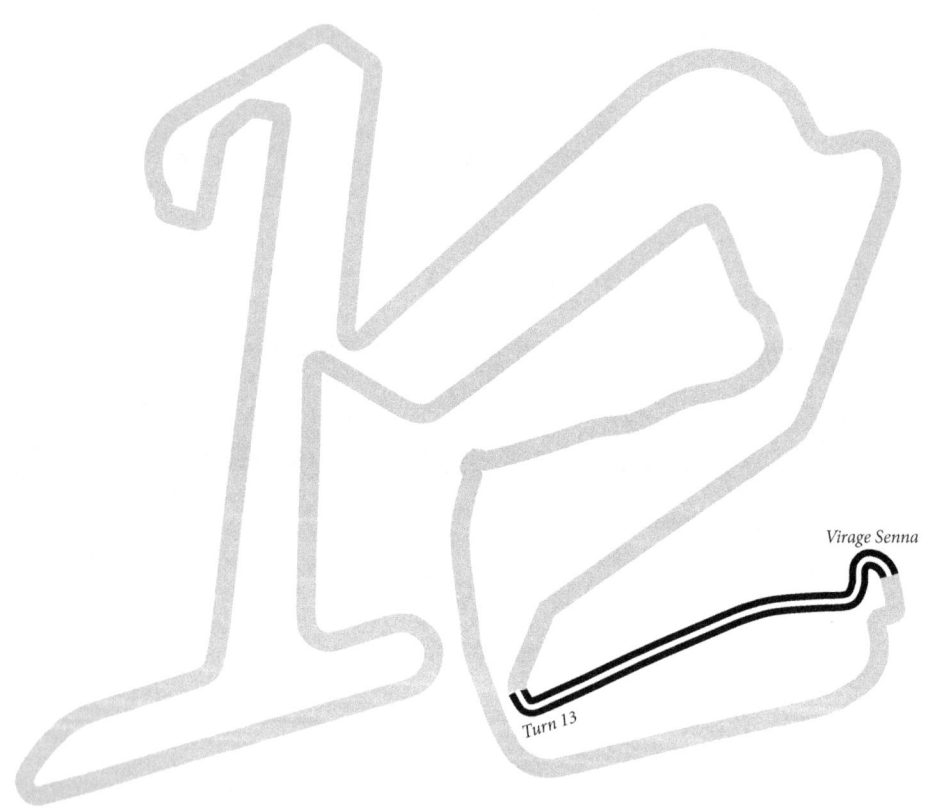

Virage Senna

Turn 13

Circuit Gilles Villeneuve

45.50182163240136, -73.52799118679674

RACE 4

2011 Canadian Grand Prix

70 Laps

"It's so wet down at the hairpin, the run off the hairpin. So so wet, you can't see anything at all, aquaplaning on the way."

The Marathon

In all professional sports, one question never ceases to be debated is comparing greatness. Who is the Greatest Of All Time, also known as the GOAT. Media loves to worship athletes onto a pedestal then throw in a few competitors to stir up the conversation. In the world of basketball, it has been a Michael Jordan and LeBron James debate for the last decade and counting; in tennis, Rod Laver and Roger Federer; in soccer, Cristiano Ronaldo and Lionel Messi; in golf, Jack Nicklaus and Tiger Woods. In the world of Formula One, Ayrton Senna, Michael Schumacher and Lewis Hamilton sit undeniably close to each other in this particular conversation.

The truth of the matter is, we will never know the answer because they breathed and raced in different eras, with different rules and technologies. Likewise, with the examples from other disciplines. The only possibility that would bring us near to a conclusion is perhaps through immersion in electronic games. We all know video games nowadays can be extremely advanced and realistic in terms of graphics and delivering an experience that matches reality. Well, at least that is the objective or the intention of the video game today. Then again, let us be reminded that it is just a simulation based on a driver's set attribute that was defined by a group of data researchers.

How one driver would fare from the other in a different era will be a mystery, like it or not. If we simplified this question and put aside the time and space issue, can the current drivers on the grid be ranked accordingly and measured? Through power ranking them by track, by season and by team. The next problem we will face is clearly the hardware with which they are equipped; after all, they are working with different machines. How do we determine whether a driver outperforms the machine or vice versa? Can we reset certain values on the machine to an extent that no one takes advantage or a head start? One comes to my mind: rain.

When raindrops land onto the tarmac, the set-up of the car has less impact, the engine power advantage is compromised and manipulated by the humidity on the track. The choice of tyre will have more power than the aerodynamic that the chassis produces. All drivers get the same set of wet tyres; intermediate or extreme wet, depending on the condition. Fair play kicks in. All the advantages one might have with their cars' engine or aero set-ups are out the window. It then comes down to a few components for the race: quick thinking from the strategists, the driver's true ability to wrestle with the wheels and race under the treacherous conditions and, last but not least, luck.

Wet races draw high ratings with anticipation of drama and suspense, hence they are highly entertaining. That is why it is far more exciting watching a wet race. At the turn of the new decade, Formula One's YouTube channel released a Top 10 Race of the decade, consisting of the highlights from the best races of the 2010-2019 seasons; not surprisingly half of them are wet races. Bernie Ecclestone, the former supremo who orchestrated the competition to become a global phenomenon, once suggested bringing an artificial wet race to spice up his competition. The idea was to sprinkle water onto the track to make the race more of a lottery for all parties. The wet race is a lottery for all drivers on the grid; positions on the grid matter less as positions can change hands corner to corner. Under the rain, everyone gets a chance at winning the Grand Prix.

The rain was what we had in store on Sunday, the 12th of June 2011. The Formula One calendar brought our attention to Montreal, Canada. Circuit Gilles Villeneuve, the backdrop for the 2011 Canadian Grand Prix, the 7th out of the 19 scheduled races in a one bull race season. That bull I am referring to was Sebastian Vettel's Red Bull RB7. The car Vettel had a love affair with so deeply was known as Kinkie Kylie. Yes, Vettel named his cars, not just this one but all his cars past and present. Vettel and Kinkie Kyle were such a great pairing, partners in crime, whatever you may want to call them; together they took home 11 winner trophies from 19 tries, somewhat unprecedented at the time.

Vettel, the reigning champion of 2010 was on the top of the podium five out of the first six races prior to Canadian Grand Prix, and the season was bordering on boredom. To add insult to injury, the cars' racing speeds took a tumble, due to new regulation banning several aero devices. The world of Formula One fans was desperately begging for a challenger sooner rather than later. They, not just the fans but I believe even Formula One itself, was praying for a messiah to save the boring and predictable season.

We all prayed. We were disappointed Vettel took pole once again in Canada on Saturday's qualifying, seizing control of the race with P1 to start the race in fresh air. We continued to pray. Come Sunday, race day, we were still unsure if Fernando Alonso who started next to Vettel will be the Messiah; if anyone, the Spaniard would be the most experienced and qualified for the role. Prayers continued with the sky overcast that turned into rain. Was this the answer from the Formula One God? Still looking uncertain, because Vettel had proved to the world when he became the youngest Formula One race winner by claiming his maiden victory two years prior, under the rain. These conditions would be far more suitable to his liking, we all sensed.

Had the saviour emerged and hidden himself under the visor? We were all anxious to find out who it might be.

The time had finally arrived, however this time, when the five lights went out, there was not any dashing to the first corner action. Instead, all cars were tamed to follow the safety car[1] that was leading and pacing as a safety measure. The rain was rowdy before the race with the track collecting enough water to warrant a safety car start. This is common practice for a wet race to avoid any major accidents or pile up with the tricky conditions. Race control knew too well from experience that, in every race start, with an adrenaline rush, it is common to see a lot of silly stuff entering the first corner. Safety car start was absolutely the right call.

That only meant, for the first couple of laps, we were watching all cars with full extreme wet tyres[2] clearing standing water from pushing hard enough to create a dry racing line together as a group. All 24 cars synchronised in action to expel as much as 65 litres of rainwater per second before racing conditions were met. After 4 laps, race control finally gave the thumbs up and racing they went.

It was Vettel, Alonso, Felipe Massa, Mark Webber, Hamilton, Nico Rosberg, Jenson Button, Michael Schumacher, Nick Heidfeld and Vitaly Petrov that raced across the start-finish line to kick off the race. All cars,

1 Safety car is the course vehicle that runs and paces as the leading car during the race in the event of a problem that requires the cars to be slowed, i.e. to allow track marshals to clear debris from an accident.

2 Extreme wet tyres sometimes refer as full wets, these tyres are designed to be used under heavy rain conditions.

bar Vettel, were driving into clouds of spray, and it quickly became apparent that it would be a long afternoon when Webber and Hamilton tangled at the first corner. Hamilton fancied his chance inside turn 1 but did not have enough momentum, under-steered[3] and clipped Webber and sent his RB7 spinning, dropping the Aussie from P4 to P14. Hamilton meanwhile lost just a spot from that ambitious move, falling behind seven-time world champion Schumacher. That was only lap 5 of the race.

For whatever reason, Hamilton seemed rather restless at the beginning of this race, and attempted to go around the outside of the hairpin[4] at turn 10, while Schumacher took a tighter line, the Brit went wide into the grass. With this impetuous move, Hamilton lost another spot, this time to his teammate Button, the former Brawn GP champion. That was only lap 6 of the race.

So what is that old saying, if at first or second you do not succeed, try again. Coming out of turn 14, Hamilton lined himself up behind Button on the straight and pulled out to his left. Button moved into his racing line ready to position his car for the right-hander entry, unaware his compatriot was at his left rear; the two touched. With the amount of the velocity generated from the straight-line speed of the Mercedes FO 108Y engine, a slight nudge forced a change of direction and proved to be lethal. The back end of Hamilton's MP4-26 brushed the pit wall, damaging the ever-so-fragile rear suspension. Race over for the 2008 world champion. That was only lap 7 of the race.

"What was he doing?!" the 2009 world champion cried over his radio. Button was upset but he was lucky his car escaped any potential race-ending damage.

In the space of three laps, Hamilton had concluded his Canadian adventure with three separate incidents, a couple of them under

3 Under-steer is a term used to explain that the front end of the car does not want to turn into a corner and slides wide as the driver tries to turn in towards the apex.

4 Hairpin is a very tight corner, usually in an angle that makes car turn almost 180° to continue on the track.

investigation by the race stewards[5], with the last one delivering the DNF next to his name. With Hamilton's damaged goods parked at turn 5, race control was forced to deploy the safety car for the second time. Time for some quick decision making by all the strategists at work; these decisions tend to make or break the race if the gamble turns in favour of their drivers.

Button was the first to make a move, diving down the pit lane and asking for the inters. Intermediate tyres are the rubber with less shallow groove for a damp track, an ideal choice for a drying circuit. Under the right conditions, inters can have 20% more grip than full wet tyres. It is always hard to be the first to put your hand up, but McLaren felt it was worth a shot. The rest of the teams would monitor the lap time by the cars that had switched to inters before making the call for their drivers. Button rejoined the track at P14, while the top three positions remained Vettel, Alonso and Massa. That was lap 9 of the race.

"Okay, Sebastian, you know we have Button, who has pitted and fitted inters. We will keep a close eye on him." Rocky, Vettel's race engineer relating the issue to his driver over the radio.

The race resumed on lap 12 once the track marshals had cleared Hamilton's car from turn 5 and the carbon fibre debris around the crime scene. Cars returned to racing when the safety car peeled off to the pit lane. To call this Canadian Grand Prix eventful is an understatement, after all, the race had not reached the quarter mark, and the next thing we knew, Button had been slapped with a drive-through penalty for speeding under the safety car.

The rule states that all cars need to keep within a certain speed limit when driving under the safety car period. Button had been pinned for going over the given limit and was penalised for a drive-through, which he served by driving his car into the pit lane in 60kph speed limit while

---

5 Stewards are officials overseeing and refereeing the Grand Prix weekend to ensure race and sessions are conducted by the regulation.

all his competition were speeding through the pit straight in the region of 250kph. This was Button's second visit to the pit lane and this penalty dropped him down to P15. It was out of the frying pan and into the fire for Button. That was lap 14 of the race.

While everyone was still waiting to see any significant gain from putting on inters, they were still nervous about the weather, as the rain had persisted as a quiet backdrop. At this point, Button was cruising, with one second faster than the leaders and making ground to P8 by lap18, so a few cars finally decided to follow suit, these included Alonso from P2. Unfortunately for Alonso, he did not benefit from the change because, less than a lap from his tyre change, the huge downpour came bucketing down onto the 4.3km circuit.

Lap 20, the safety car was deployed for the third occasion, while both Alonso and Button took the opportunity to switch back to full wets. Both rejoined the race P8 and P12 respectively. For your information, this was Button's third trip to the pit lane. While, for the front runners Vettel, Kobayashi and Massa, the trio was very fortunate to be patient with the tyre game and got a free pit stop during the safety car period. All had a fresh set of full wets to counter the heavy rain that was making cars aquaplane[6]. Visibility became increasingly difficult and dangerous.

"Just for your information, from turn 9 to turn 13 is undrivable. It's undrivable!" Vettel reported to his team to share the track condition.

"It's so wet down at the hairpin, the run off the hairpin. So so wet, you can't see anything at all, aquaplaning on the way." Button concurred with the condition.

With conditions not improving, Charlie Whiting, the race director, made the call to red-flag and suspended the race until further notice. The race

6 Aquaplane is a state where tyre failed to generate grip or make contact to the wet surface of the tarmac, resulting in car sliding out of control.

was effectively suspended on lap 25 for a good two hours by the forces of nature. Fans were reminded of the last red-flagged event due to heavy rain in Malaysia 2009. This particular Sunday probably had been more of a deja vu for most drivers, dealing with safety car interventions one after another. The race finally resumed under the safety car from lap 26, this time for 9 laps before allowing the cars behind to get on racing again on lap 35, just reaching the halfway mark of the 70 lap race.

As soon as the race returned to full green lights, a train of cars streaked down the pit lane for the inters again as the sky cleared, with an obvious drying track emerging. This included Button, who was making his fourth pit lane visit for the afternoon. A lap later, the second group of cars came in for the same reason, including all front runners except for race leaders Vettel and Kobayashi. The two Ferraris had to double-stack[7] for a tyre change; this dropped Alonso further down the field when he rejoined the race. While the commentators were all wondering when Vettel would pit for fresh rubber, the TV director had our attention on a Ferrari beached on turn 3 and 4 chicane[8].

It was Alonso, and his Ferrari F150 was stationery on the green with the track marshal at the rear of the car signalling assistance, yellow flag flashing, signifying another safety car deployment. This was only lap 37, and the safety car was out and about for the fifth time for the race and second time in the space of two laps. The replay showed Button and Alonso coming together at the chicane, ending the double world champion's race, with Button nursing a tyre puncture.

Insanely, for the fifth time, Button headed back to the pit lane as carefully as the bank guards its gold, not wanting to further damage his car or the delicate suspension that was still holding the broken tyre. The only consolation that came out of that pit stop was that his car was still healthy,

7 Double-stack refers to team pitting both their drivers together and they had to queue up to be serviced.
8 Chicane a tight sequence of corners in alternate directions.

and they rolled their dice for dry slick tyres. Again, the first car to make the significant move at the time of the race. What was there to lose? He was dead last.

The game plan for the McLaren team was damage limitation with their only car running solo, relegated to P21. They would be happy if Button could salvage some championship points, if any. Any point would be a win from now on, with 33 laps remaining. Meanwhile, Vettel took advantage of yet another free pit stop from the safety car, to maintain his P1 status. The young German was just so invincible in this condition and this race. No drivers had come close enough to challenge his lead after so many stops and restarts. It looked as though there was no messiah to the rescue. Not in Canada at least!

In the next 15 laps, it was racing at its best, with so many battles throughout the drying circuit. By lap 55, it was Vettel, Schumacher and Webber to round off the top three drivers. The fastest car on the track was, however, not among the top three drivers, but the car that was running fourth; surprise surprise - Jenson Button! I did not know how, black magic perhaps, Button had darted through the field and made up 17 places in the space of 15 laps. With another 15 laps remaining, podium finish looked vastly possible after overcoming all the cars he had to pass.

Life Lesson #4

Dancing in the Rain

The gamble had paid dividends for Button and his team with dry slick tyres, clocking fastest laps one after another, moving him behind fellow friend Webber and 20 seconds from the race leader Vettel. Before we knew it, yet another safety car was issued for clearing the debris left behind by Heidfeld's Renault. That was lap 57, which bunched up all the cars, with Vettel, Schumacher, Webber, and Button all following behind each other.

The race resumed on lap 61, where Vettel ran away to build another healthy lead, leaving the trio, Schumacher, Webber and Button battling it out amongst themselves for a few good laps. Webber ran wide through the chicane and Button quickly capitalised on podium position from the Australian on lap 65. Before the end of that lap, Button made a move with DRS assistance to pass the rain master Schumacher for P2. With that promotion, the 2009 world champion was just a couple of seconds behind race leader Vettel, with 5 laps before the chequered flag. By this pace, Button could catch Vettel in a matter of a few laps. Catching Vettel is one thing, passing him is another story altogether. Anyone from the McLaren camp would be happy with the P2 result, after all, Button had surged all the way from the back. P2 was considered an overachievement, the last thing on his mind was to throw it all away with a silly move on Vettel.

After more than 4 hours, the race had come to the final lap, with just 0.6 second separating 2009 and 2010 world champions; it was nerve-wracking. Button was hunting down Vettel, without showing any signs of desperation, still super smooth with all his turns. When it seemed Vettel had it all covered, his wheel marginally brushed the damp tarmac, and the moisture was enough for his car to lose the grip it needed to keep it on the track. Vettel went wide on turn 6, Button danced passed the championship leader and led for the remaining eight corners; the only time he had led the race and the only lap that really mattered. Button completed his comeback by crossing the chequered flag for the longest Formula One race in history. The enthralling race that was well deserved to be dubbed as the race of the decade.

Life is full of obstacles, bumps, hiccups, ups and downs, and whatever comes with them. We are exposed to constant turbulence, much like a race where we will face safety cars, penalties and accidents that are going to put us down. For Button, the early contact with teammates did not matter, he kept going. The drive-through penalty was out of his control and did not bother him, he kept his head down. The sudden downpour that forced him to change tyres did not annoy him, he kept persevering. The damage he sustained from the on-track accident which relegated him to the back did not demoralise him, he kept fighting. Never at any point during the race, he or the team thought of calling it a day. They kept themselves in the game despite all the punches being thrown at them.

When life throws us lemons, make lemonade. Life is not about waiting for the storm to pass, it is about learning to dance in the rain. At times it might seem impossible to dig ourselves out of the hole, but do not give up. It might seem we have just entered the darkness and the end of the tunnel is too far to comprehend, keep walking. It might seem the silver lining would never appear after the storm, keep praying. It might seem we are on the way from rebounding from setbacks only to find out otherwise, stand back up. It might seem like everything in life is going wrong, we still need to keep our heads held high and keep trying. Do not let the rain, the safety car, the accidents, the penalties in your life stop you from getting to the chequered flag. Keep racing.

> *"No matter how many mistakes you make or how slow you progress, you are still way ahead of everyone who isn't trying."*
> Anthony Robbins

At various times, you might need to reassess the objectives of the life you are racing for. At P21, a race win might not have been a realistic goal for Button, he was just taking it lap by lap to see where he could end up in.

Sometimes the win does not lie in the race victory, but never lose sight of where you intend to go in the first place.

Luck Favours Perseverance

Was Button lucky to have won the Canadian Grand Prix? Yes and no. Luck was always needed in any wet race when unpredictability was at stake. To play devil's advocate, the six safety car periods had helped and also worked against his favour. We could easily argue that it was Vettel's mistake that granted Button's win. But let's remember, Button never threw in the towel, even when he found himself right at the back of all the cars. He weathered the storm and positioned himself for the race win. Had he not pushed to get behind Vettel, he would never have had the opportunity to seize the lead when Vettel cracked under pressure. Button proved it is not how you start the race but how you finish. His supremacy and wet weather prowess had set himself up for glory. It was a well-deserved win for Button; he had ticked all the boxes for the win, if not more.

> *"The Luck thing - really there is no such things as good luck, it's good preparation and hard work."*
>
> Bruce McLaren

If we want luck in our life, we need to position ourselves for it. Good fortunate is not going to come at us when we are not ready to receive it at the right timing. If we want to finish the race, we need to keep racing and clock the necessary mileage. If we want to get on the podium, we need to pick our battles. If we want to win the race, we need to play the long game and be ready for the right opportunity to pounce. No one can tell us when that is going to come, but I know we need to believe and keep our engines going and persevere. The race win is worth the wait. Just ask Jenson Button, the 2011 Canadian Grand Prix winner.

FUN FACTS ON WET RACES

The rain separates the good from the great. It is the reason drivers like Michael Schumacher (19), Lewis Hamilton (16), Ayrton Senna (14) and Jenson Button (7) were able to rack up victories under wet weather conditions, and rank higher on my all-time drivers list. Senna, namely, was outright fast in wet races. In 1984, when a 20-year-old Senna was only a rookie driving for a midfield Toleman team, he showed the world what he could do with his sub-par machine. In the sixth Grand Prix of his career, under the rain at the most challenging circuit on the calendar in terms of overtaking, Senna's brilliance in the wet was a showstopper on the streets of Monaco. Starting 13th and picking his way through, he was on the tail of the race leader Alain Prost's McLaren in only 29 laps. He could easily have challenged for the win had the race not been red-flagged and suspended due to the conditions. Likewise, a heroic performance by the great Schumacher in the 1996 Spanish Grand Prix distinguished himself from the rest, earning his nickname "rain master".

WATCH

2007 European Grand Prix, 2011 Canadian Grand Prix, 2016 Brazilian Grand Prix.

DID YOU KNOW

Jensen Button has achieved 15 wins and 50 podiums in his career but has never stepped onto the podium in his home race at the British Grand Prix? He finished P4 twice in 2004 and 2014.

Casino Triangle

Turn 1

Suzuka International Racing Course

34.84577840688797, 136.53902730181585

RACE 5

2012 Japanese Grand Prix

53 Laps

"Kamui! Kamui! Kamui!...."

The Rising Son

Formula One, the pinnacle of motorsport is every bit about competitions. Millions of fans from all over the world tune in or turn up for the juicy competitions amongst the top 20 drivers, battling to be the quickest man on earth. It is all about competition for the fans and winning races for the drivers. Winning is everything. Competitive nature lived in all the drivers even before they were born. Many of them carried genes from their ancestry, mixed from amateur and professional motorsport greats. The Hills, The Villeneuves, The Rosbergs are all father and son world champion pairings, with the racing DNA running in the family blood. To say they were born to win is an understatement. Winning already started way before birth.

The 2012 season proved to be a season that produced winners. Multiple winners. Multiple winners from the past, and winners for the future to come. Before the season-opening race in Melbourne on March 18th, there were six world champions suited up for the 20-race calendar. At the time, Sebastian Vettel, Fernando Alonso, Kimi Räikkönen, Lewis Hamilton,

Jenson Button and Michael Schumacher had a combined 14 world titles under their belts. It was a season where we got to witness battles between the crème de la crème, and with that came high expectations.

What we got in return was an unprecedented record for the books, with the first seven races producing seven different winners. One surprising race winner after another, with no repeat winners when the first third of the season had been completed. Unpredictability. Exactly what the 500 million Formula One fans worldwide were, and still are, hoping for. We never wanted a one horse-race, no puns intended, we always long for competition. The season delivered nail biters and produced one of the most climacteric seasons in recent history. Winning in the most dramatic and entertaining fashion.

Round 15, we found ourselves in the land of the rising sun, the Japanese Grand Prix at the classic circuit of Suzuka. This was the second race of the Asian leg in which I got to enjoy watching the race on TV, with little time difference. Japan was only an hour ahead of Malaysia, where I resided at the time. While being an Asian by birth, I faced some predicament in choosing the drivers or the team to follow. It is only natural that I lean towards drivers who share the same or similar background. Japanese culture sits close to my heart, and to have a driver who represents Japan is a somewhat proud association. Since 2006, the year I embarked on my Formula One journey, there have been very few Japanese drivers that stack up; Tukama Sato, Kazuki Nakajima just to name a few. One shining star that caught the attention of many, including me, was a lad called Kamui Kobayashi.

Kobayashi first came under the limelight of Formula One when he was a reserve driver at Panasonic Toyota Racing in 2007. Serving as a test driver[1], he had worked diligently in the background for a solid two years for the Japanese squad. He got his first nod to race in the 2009 Brazilian

---

1 Test driver is a racing driver contracted by the team to be involved in the development and testing of the car. They are also known as reserve drivers, when called upon duty to race if the team's lead driver is unable to compete due to injury, sanctioned by FIA or personal reasons.

Grand Prix, a penultimate round of the season when Timo Glock, the second driver for the team, had suffered an injury from the previous outing. Kobayashi started P11 on the grid and finished P9, just missing out on scoring his first championship point[2] in his debut race. He did, however, finish ahead of his more experienced compatriot Nakajima of the AT&T Williams. Kobayashi wasted no time in seizing his chance, and landed his maiden points in the following race in Abu Dhabi just weeks later. Qualified P12 and finished the race at P6 ahead of his veteran teammate Jarno Trulli.

With such a result, I was expecting the young Japanese to land a full-time role with the team. Unfortunately, just three weeks from the conclusion of the Brazilian Grand Prix, Toyota announced they were pulling out the sport, ending their eight years of involvement and development with Formula One. At the same time ending Kobayashi's shot at the seat to race for his beloved country.

They say when one door closes, another window opens. Fittingly so for Kobayashi; he secured his next employment with the BMW Sauber Formula One Team as their second driver. He was quickly promoted to first driver after easily out-scoring his more experienced teammates in Pedro Del la Rosa and Nick Heidfeld in his first year with the Swiss team by a huge margin of 32 to 14 in championship points. Proven to be a driver who delivers results, Kobayashi scored 120 career championship points before the 2012 Japanese Grand Prix; an overachievement, considering he had been driving with mediocre machines during the four-year stint with Toyota and Sauber.

With his home Grand Prix in his sights, he was destined to achieve more than what he was given. Not every driver on the grid has the privilege to be racing in front of his home crowd, and the pressure to deliver great results can sometimes put them under the pump. For example, Mark

2 Championship points in season 2009 were awarded to the top 8 drivers only. With the distribution of 10, 8, 6, 5, 4, 3, 2, 1.

Webber and Daniel Ricciardo have never stepped on the podium in their home race in Australia. Between the two Aussies, they have a combined seven retirements, four non-scoring finishes, and the best result was P4 in 20 Grand Prix entries. It is never as easy as it seems; to be able to achieve point finish, podium or race victory required many factors to turn in their favour. There are many variables, they need to have the right car, strategy, conditions and circumstances to bid for great outcomes.

> *"I am proud to go home and race there, this is certain. It is both – a lot more pleasurable and extra pressure."*
> Kamui Kobayashi

The Japanese Grand Prix was Kobayashi's race. It always was. Racing at home in front of his countrymen was such a privilege; this was especially true as Asian drivers are a minority in motorsports. The 2012 Japanese Grand Prix felt like a chance of a lifetime for Kobayashi, as he managed to outperform his Sauber C31 by putting it on the second row of the grid from Saturday's awesome qualifying performance. It was certainly a treat for all Japanese, young and old, at the Suzuka International Racing Course as well as those millions rooting for the home hero from their TV. This kind of opportunity does not come often in life and Kobayashi nailed it when it mattered. This was his chance to stamp his name in the history books, where only one of the 17 Japanese drivers who ever graced Formula One came home with a podium finish. A race win was possible but not likely. With the production from his machine, a podium would be an overachievement, while solid point scoring was a realistic goal.

On Sunday 7th of October at 3pm local time, all the mechanics cleared the track except for the four who were guarding the tyre blanket[3] for each

3 Tyre blanket is also known as tyre warmer. By the name, it is designed to keep the tyre warm to their optimum operating temperature before the car takes to the track.

car. They looked anxiously at the clock, waiting for the last moment to give the tyre the heat they needed before lift-off. All cars fired up and began to weave to generate heat to their tyres. Upon completion of the formation lap, all 24 cars had found their grid positions. In order, Sebastian Vettel, Webber, Kobayashi, Romain Grosjean, Sergio Pérez, Fernando Alonso, Kimi Räikkönen, Jenson Button, Lewis Hamilton and Felipe Massa would round off the top 10. Kobayashi probably had been waiting for this time since growing up as a kid; he was as ready as he would ever be. The red lights fired up one after another and then, a second in between, lights out! Clutch off, throttles, and just as he had rehearsed time after time, his car streaked down the straight and he overtook Webber for P2 even before they reached the first braking point. It was a tardy getaway from the Australian but a Godzilla start for the Japanese star. The crowd went berserk as all the front runners found their braking point for the first turn. A good beginning makes a good ending.

Not so much of a good beginning for several cars entering turn 1; mayhem claimed Nico Rosberg instantaneously, while Bruno Senna of Williams, Grosjean of Lotus, Webber of Red Bull were all forced into the pits to replace their $150,000.00 front wings. But the biggest victim was none other than Alonso; his Ferrari F2012 was clipped and spun out of the race by Lotus's Räikkönen. Alonso's current 29 championship point lead was in serious jeopardy as his main rival Vettel could capitalise by winning the race that afternoon, erasing the lead to merely four points with five races to play for.

With Vettel having all the motivation now to take home the 25 championship points, he pulled away from Kobayashi with a 5-second gap in 10 laps, setting purple sectors[4] one after another. For Kobayashi, it was not about keeping pace with the race leader, but keeping away from the cars behind, namely Button and Massa. Button was the first of

---

4 Purple sector or purple lap is the fastest time for that sector or the whole lap of all drivers who have recorded times up to that point in a session.

the frontrunners to pit for fresh rubber on lap 14 with Kobayashi trying to cover any potential undercut[5] a lap later. Staying ahead of Button was crucial to keep track position after the first stint[6] with the soft tyres, however, he found himself behind Ricciardo's Toro Rosso, and perhaps took one corner too many to dispose of the young Aussie. Coming around the last corner to start his 18th lap, Massa came out of his pit stop and snatched P2 from Kobayashi. Now P3, back to where he had started on the grid, it felt like the good work had been undone, and tension began to emerge within the sea of the red and white grandstand. Can the hometown hero hold on for another 35 laps? Just 35 laps.

"Okay Jenson, this pace is good, Kobayashi there for the taking." Button's race engineer radio message was played back on the broadcast during lap 28.

Button was being told Kobayashi's P3 was up for grabs, as the team urged the British world champion to push and close in on the Japanese. Sauber made the first move by asking Kobayashi to come in for the last round of pit stops on lap 31, to ready him for the remaining laps, while McLaren was asking Button to stick with plan B and run two laps longer in the current stint than scheduled in attempt to leapfrog Kobayashi. That did not work out for Button as planned, he overshot his pit box by centimetres, causing his crew to compromise their position for the tyre change. This mistake seemed minimal on TV, delaying the process by milliseconds, but proved to be vital as he rejoined the race 5 seconds behind the Japanese hopeful.

With the race leader sprinting away and opening up a huge gap, the TV director did not bother giving him or Massa any attention. All eyes were on the battle of the final podium place between Kobayashi and Button. Both hometown favourites in some way, Button had a huge fan base in Japan and dubbed the Japanese Grand Prix as his second home race due to his

5 Undercut is a strategy by which teams attempt to get their driver ahead of their rivals by pitting earlier to gain an advantage performance through fresh new tyres.
6 Stint refers to the phase of the race between the pit stops.

romantic relationship with local fashion model Jessica Michibata. He was known as a Japanese son-in-law. In this race though, there was no doubt who the Japanese were favouring.

Button, the 2011 winner in Japan, claimed Suzuka to be his favourite track, and his healthy record speaks for itself. He had around 16 laps to hunt down Kobayashi, and the coverage ultimately shifted heavily to this duel; it was Kobayashi's race to lose. Lap by lap, Button was making progress in lap times versus the car in front. He was coming on strongly, and he could smell blood. Kobayashi had to respond if he wanted to make history, so he did, trading personal best time with the car behind. With just a handful of laps remaining, they were only seconds apart. The intense battle had my heart racing in the range of 120bmp and, as the pair sped through the high G-force corner of the famously 130R, I was panicky as to whether the Japanese hopeful could withstand the pressure, physically and mentally. The crowds were getting twitchy too, seeing the white Sauber passing by the grandstand followed by the silver McLaren, inching his way, bridging the gap. They could see the gaps just as Kobayashi could see Button in his mirror. It was intense for all parties concerned.

Button's eyes lit up as he came into Kobayashi's DRS zone[7] and made full use of his advantage, but the Japanese was having none of it, countering moves with his use of KERS to provide a boost in the critical spot on the track. On the penultimate lap, they were just a car length apart. Vettel and Massa crossed the chequered flag and the sea of red and white could not care less. They waited for their white car to come around the final corner and they made sure he was still in front of the silver car when he passed the man waving the chequered flag.

And he did, to the crowd's delight, sending them into ecstasy.

---

7 DRS Zone(s) are sections of the circuit that is designed to allow cars to utilise their Drag Reduction System to gain advantage performance over the car in front. These zones are usually placed in long straight lines to encourage overtaking opportunities.

Japanese easily are the most passionate and creative bunch you can find among all Formula One tracks. You can easily spot the fanatical Japanese fan flocking onto the circuit with their innovative and wacky headgear and outfits; just one of their ways to show their love and passion in the sport. As soon as the gates were opened for the annual event, they filled the grandstands on Thursday when all the mechanics were preparing the cars, and the grandstand would remain packed on Sunday after the race and the ceremony. That year, Japanese grandstands waited for 56 laps, the Suzuka track waited for more than 20 years[8] to witness history in the making. They were restless, and they were on their feet chanting in a symphony for their samurai.

"Kamui! Kamui! Kamui!..." a sweet sound echoing from the main grandstand in front of the rostrum.

I was thrilled watching the race unpack itself thousands of miles away in the same continent. I thought, every dog has his day and it might as well be at the place that meant the most to him. He did it. Car number 14. The man with racing in his blood. The man racing with Japanese blood. He won. He won their hearts. He was the winner in their eyes. His name was Kamui.

Life Lesson #5

Born Winners

In life, we are all born winners, and when I say we are, I mean you and I, not just the successful athletes we have been talking about in this book. We are born winners and we are all special, unique individuals. We are born winners by science. By the principle of probability, the chances of

8 Aguri Suzuki is the first Japanese Formula One driver to step on the podium. He achieved this by finishing 3rd in his home soil during the 1990 Japanese Grand Prix.

your birth to this world are 400 trillion to 1. That is a lot of zeros, 14 to be precise. 1: 400,000,000,000,000 is the odds scientists and mathematicians have worked out for you and I to be here, wherever we are right now. Based on the probability of your parents meeting and mating in a world of seven billion others; that is the odds considering various possible factors.

So how much is 400 trillion? It is too big to comprehend for someone who struggles with numeracy like me. Let me share this concept of 400 trillion. Australia's lottery giant, The Lotts, subsidiary of the Tatts Group, is known for their extensive range of lottery games and products; Powerball, Oz Lotto, TattsLotto just to name a few. While I am not condoning gambling, please gamble responsibly. By calculation, to win a jackpot from a popular product such as Powerball works out to be 1: 292,201,338. That is the slimmest chance in life if ever one got that lucky. Let me present you with another statistic for comparison; the chance of getting struck by lightning in one's lifetime is about 1: 3,000. In other words, a person is subject to

more chances of being struck by lightning, touch wood, than winning jackpot lotto in his or her lifetime. Not to say it is impossible, it is just a lot more than a fat chance. If we think winning the lottery is hard, our birth is the biggest win we have in comparison. That is why births are celebrated.

"You are one amazing person."
Mel Robbins

Your First Race Win

We are winners as we open our eyes in the morning to welcome and embrace a brand new day. You and I have won another day by not simply surviving but living and staying in this race. We have won by giving ourselves the opportunity of what is to come for the next second, the very next minute, the coming hours till the day calls it a day. Yes, we may not win all the battles that come through on a day-to-day basis. There will be races we are just not supposed to win, but keeping yourself in it gives you the chance. Whining and bitching about our life, what we lost or what we do not have is an irresponsible act. I understand if this was just an occasional gateway, but not when complaints become a norm. Society or the world has changed so much in the last 20 years that we have created spaces for all kinds of needs. We see social media being a platform for users to abuse or vent anger, frustration and stress, some to seek attention or other intentions. If we are one that complains about our life for the sake of doing so, then we should not have won the first race of our life. We chose to compete in the race against 100 million other sperms. We did not have to win that race, but since we did, we have to act like a winner.

We are all winners in our own way, in our own right, in our own family, groups and communities. Just like Kobayashi, he was a winner for his people. He will always be remembered as a winner, in that race and his achievement through the sports community. His name was not

only cemented as a winner but also as a corner. Turn 11 of the Suzuka
Racing Circuit was named 'Kobayashi Corner' after he had made
some extraordinary overtaking manoeuvres, passing five drivers with his
aggressive moves in the 2010 version of the Japanese Grand Prix.

"Run your own race, you can't lose."
Rolf Dobelli

Winning has a different interpretation in Formula One. Every team
approaches their wins differently. Having different starting points grants
the team to have different targets and expectations. That is to say, we
never expect backmarkers such as HASS, Alfa Romeo or Williams to
have a crack at race victory anytime soon in the year 2020. Finishing in
points will be considered a win for any of these teams, as they are the
real targets. Midfield teams are expected to challenge for positions of the

third-best cars, behind Mercedes and Red Bull. McLaren, Ferrari, Renault, AlphaTauri are teams aiming for podium positions. For them, regular visits to the podium will be considered a great success. Mercedes are expected to win every week based on their dominant trend since the Hybrid era, with Red Bull the only real contender to put up a decent fight every now and then. They are the two teams expected to collect most of the silverware every race. Kobayashi's Sauber in 2012 was nothing more than a car keeping its head above the water in the mix of fierce midfield competition. His podium was a win for the team no doubt.

> *"The two most important days in your life are the day you are born and the day you find out why."*
>
> Mark Twain

Kobayashi brought the house down in Suzuka, but he could not keep his Sauber seat after delivering such a solid result for the Swiss-based team, and regretfully he was let go. His Formula One career continued with one more year in the lowly team of Caterham Formula One Racing before moving on to other motorsport competitions. Life after Formula One saw the Japanese talent triumph in the 24 Hours of Daytona in 2019 and 2020 under the WeatherTech SportsCar Championship. As of today, Kamui Kobayashi is leading the FIA World Endurance Championship with 112 points and two race wins next to his name, and I truly believe the wins will continue to come his way because, like all of us, he is a born winner.

> *"I am not designed to come second or third. I am designed to win."*
>
> Ayrton Senna

FUN FACTS ON JAPANESE GRAND PRIX

The Japanese Grand Prix has been a favourite among the drivers and also a crowd-pleaser. The host served up some of the best title showdowns, crowning 13 world champions on Japanese soil, including five from the late 80s to early 90s. From 1988 to 1990, it delivered epic season finales between the legendary rivalry of Frenchman Alain Prost and Brazilian Ayrton Senna. The trilogy produced mixed feelings for both camps. Senna's first world championship in 1988 will always be remembered as one of the worthy races, while the following two years ended in the most controversial fashion one can imagine. The collision prematurely ended the campaign before the chequered flag on both occasions. Alessandro Nannini of Benetton was the beneficiary of the 1989 season finale that saw Senna disqualified from the race with his altercation with Prost, prompting the Italian racer to achieve his solo victory in his cut-short career.

WATCH

2008 British Grand Prix, 2012 Japanese Grand Prix, 2012 European Grand Prix.

DID YOU KNOW

Kamui Kobayashi would become a sushi chef in Japan had he not made it to the racing scene?

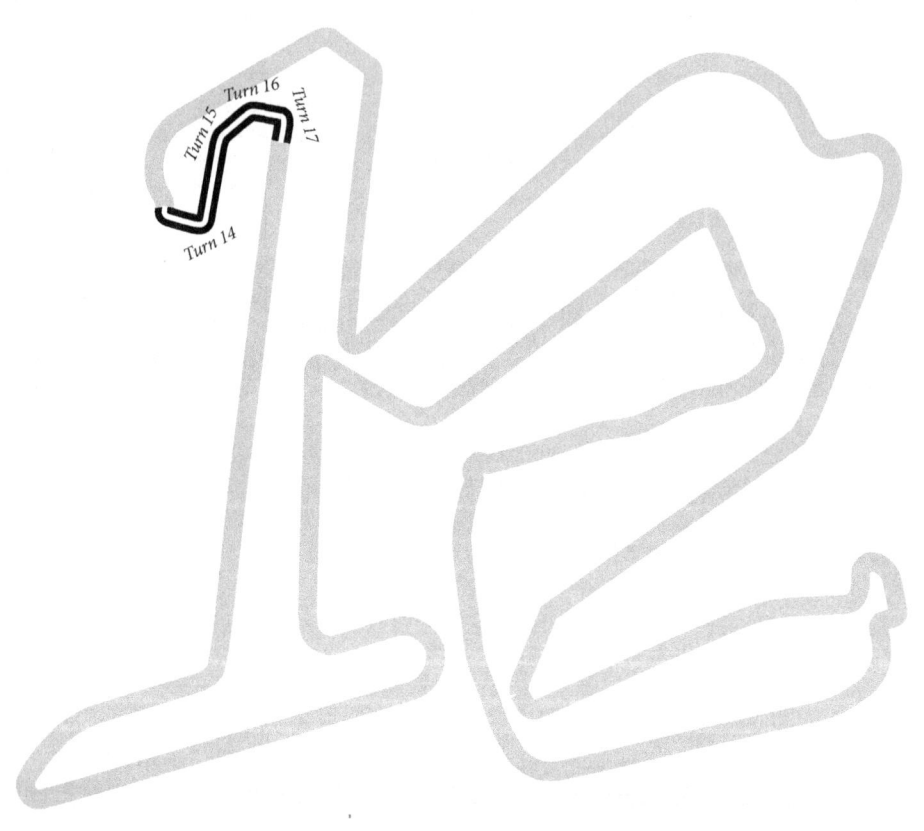

Turn 15
Turn 16
Turn 17
Turn 14

Yas Marina Circuit

24.475266647196836, 54.60392534988279

RACE 6

2012 Abu Dhabi Grand Prix

55 Laps

"Leave me alone, I know what I am doing."

The Jewel of Formula One

Weeks after the 2012 Japanese Grand Prix, we found ourselves at the final race of the Asian leg, the jewel of the desert, the Abu Dhabi Grand Prix. The tables had turned with Sebastian Vettel now leading the championship standings with 240 points to Fernando Alonso's 227. At one stage during the season, Alonso was leading by as much as 40 points over his closest rival. The DNF from the Japanese Grand Prix was costly and now was hurting the Spanish champion to play catch up for the last three races; Abu Dhabi, United States and the season finale at Sao Paulo, Brazil. Of course, Alonso was still very much in the hunt, momentum could switch either way in a matter of a few races, or even a few corners. For the fans, that was what we wanted to see, a title showdown right to the very last race. I had previously witnessed the championship being won on the very last corner of the very last race. It was as epic as anyone could have scripted. I believed the 2012 season was heading in the right direction to provide the excitement and climax just as the seasons in 2007 and 2008 had done.

Before that, though, Alonso needed to get past Abu Dhabi; a track that did not bring many fond memories for him. The 2010 race was still fairly fresh to my memory, as it had provided a dramatic ending to the season. The cruel reality of all competitive sports is that there can only be one winner and, on the day, Alonso had all the odds to win the world title in 2010 at the Yas Marina Circuit. He did not. As talented as he is as a racing legend, that fateful night saw him caught behind Vitaly Petrov of Renault during the crucial moments of the year. His fate was sealed behind the Renault R30, thus handing the championship to the 23-year-old Vettel on the last day of the season. It was not a defeat that Alonso could take on the chin.

Fast-tracking back to 2012, when qualifying was done and dusted on Saturday evening, I sensed that things could be different this time around. Alonso's qualifying result landed him at P6. Vettel had his Red Bull RB8, aka Abbey, three places ahead of his rival in P3 but that was short-lived. FIA imposed a penalty to Vettel when his car ran out of fuel and was unable to provide the 1-litre fuel sample[1] for post-qualifying scrutiny. His qualifying time was subsequently dismissed and he was sent to the back of the grid for the Sunday night race. This relegation meant a great deal for Alonso's championship campaign, now with 13 points deficit, he was in prime position to make up for lost ground. The context made the race alive once again and the bookies were busy updating odds for the punters.

On race day, Sunday 5th of November, Red Bull had opted to run Vettel from the pit lane to start the race, to avoid any potential carnage through the first few corners. The goal for him was clearly damage limitation, to run a longer stint with medium Pirellis to make up places and salvage championship points, if any were on offer. While Vettel and Abbey were stationary at the pit exit, other drivers took their cars on the formation lap, crisscrossing through the marvels of the architecture at Yas Marina Circuit. The glamour and glitter of Abu Dhabi all reflected onto the 22 cars[2] that were finding their way to the lights. The cars succumbed to their slot and lined up on the grid in order. Lewis Hamilton, Mark Webber, Pastor

1 Fuel sampling as mandated in Article 6.6.2 of the technical regulations: "Competitors must ensure that a 1-litre sample of fuel may be taken from the car at any time during the event.

2 Only 22 cars lined up on the grid with Vettel and Pedro de la Rosa of HRT opted to start their race from the pitlane.

Maldonado, Kimi Räikkönen, Jenson Button, Alonso, Nico Rosberg, Felipe Massa, Romain Grosjean and Nico Hülkenberg rounded off the top 10 drivers on the grid. They waited for the five red lights before them and it was the green lights for Vettel to officially get the race underway.

All lights out, the cars were scanning around to find gaps and spaces through the acceleration of their V8 engines, from left to right or whichever way worked for them. Webber was slow to launch his car, allowing Räikkönen to pip him for P2 going into the first turn. The Australian dropped a handful of places, as a nanosecond delay on the track can translate to a decent amount of places lost in a blink of an eye. After surviving lap 1, Hamilton led from Räikkönen, Maldonado, Alonso, Webber, Button, Massa, Kobayashi, Pérez and Schumacher, while Vettel was busy making up places from the back.

The safety car was brought out on lap 9 after Rosberg was caught out when Karthikeyan's HRT suffered from hydraulic[3] failure, causing his car to slow down without warning. Rosberg had no time to react and launched over the HRT and was airborne for a good second before the velocity carried the car and slammed sideways into the barrier. Carbon fibre from both cars exploded and scattered on turn 15 and 16. Both cars were deemed terminal, however the drivers escaped unharmed, thanks to the safety features in the modern Formula One cars. Vettel meanwhile had an eventful race, thus far damaging his front wing on two separate occasions; one in the early battle with Bruno Senna, the other, a lapse of concentration during the safety car period when he was captured running into the polystyrene bollard. He pitted for the new front wings and had his work cut out, finding himself in familiar territory again at the back of the field.

Lap 20, with 21 cars still fighting it out under the power of the street lights, one of the cars found itself with no power to continue. It was neither

3 Hydraulic is systems that oversee and controls applications, including ABS and power-assisted braking; clutch, gearbox, and throttle actuation; and controlling engine air inlets and active suspensions.

Vettel nor Alonso, the two title contenders, but race leader Hamilton of McLaren. His Mercedes powered MP4-27 had thrown in the towel early, just like his championship campaign for the year. The car was in neutral gear and the driver shook his head helplessly as he and his car rolled onto the grass to submit themselves to defeat. This was Hamilton's fifth DNF for the season, clearly, 2012 was a year to forget for the 2008 world champion.

This retirement meant Hamilton had handed the race leading position to the 2007 world champion Kimi Räikkönen of Lotus Racing. Now, a bit of context here for both the team and the driver. Lotus Formula One Team was previously known as Renault Racing prior to 2010. As Lotus, they had yet to taste success on the track or race victory since their predecessor had achieved back-to-back drivers' and constructors' world championships in 2005 and 2006. The man behind the wheel who helped the team to achieve that feat was the young Fernando Alonso. The man behind the current wheel for the Lotus team, Kimi Räikkönen, won his one and only world championship in 2007, as a Ferrari driver, and his last win was in 2009 Belgian Grand Prix, his last year with the Italian squad. He had since taken a two-year sabbatical from Formula One to race in the World Rally Championship[4], a completely different motorsport competition. At the time of writing this book, he is still the last Ferrari world champion.

Räikkönen's return to Formula One in 2012 was welcome news for the competition and very much to a fan like myself. Signing with Lotus, who had little backing with a winning package, had the paddock talking and doubting. The Finn quickly put people's doubts behind him with his driving, in typical Kimi fashion. Scoring six podiums before the Abu Dhabi Grand Prix, showing he had not lost a beat after being away from a Formula One cockpit for two years. His next goal was obvious; to deliver a race win for the British outfit. His chance was 35 laps away. We all know way too well a lot can happen in 35 laps, as we have learned from the past chapters.

4 The World Rally Championship (WRC) is a rallying series that competes on surfaces ranging from gravel, tarmac and snow. The driver paired with a co-driver competes in stages with a 1.6-litre four-cylinder car.

Nothing is certain until the driver crosses the chequered flag, and even after the race, the results can still sometimes be subject to scrutiny, appeal and stewards' decision based on circumstances. The Lotus team, including the race team principal, engineers, mechanics and strategists had every reason to be nervous for the remaining laps. To make sure they have given everything to their lead driver at his disposal and put him in the box seat for the race victory. To feed him information on track condition, telemetry from his car, performance from the rivals and so much more. They knew Räikkönen had all it takes to win, but they just needed to make sure they had done their best from their end.

"Okay Kimi, next guy behind you is Alonso. Alonso 5 seconds behind you. I will keep you updated on the gap, I will keep you updated with the pace." Räikkönen's race engineer Mark Slade voiced his update.

"Leave me alone, I know what I am doing!" Räikkönen reminded him who was the driver.

Sometimes the driver indeed knew better. Like I said before in the earlier chapter, Formula One is a sport that requires the driver and the car to be one complete athlete. It is about the partnership with the car, the bonding relationship transforming man and machine in perfect harmony. They are inseparable. Räikkönen knew all too well at the time what he needed to do with his Lotus E20. He just needed his race engineer to bugger off so he could do what he does best, driving the car fast. Not driving a fast car, because his E20 simply was not the fastest car in 2012, but he knew how to make it faster. Pushing the right buttons, finding the limits of the machine, just like any Formula One great would do, to make it quicker.

Lap 39 saw another crash that involved Pérez, Grosjean and Webber, resulting in the second safety car period for the night. Grosjean and Webber were both victimised by Pérez's negligence, ending their race with both cars damaged, while Pérez had a lucky escape. The race was neutralised with Räikkönen's 9-second lead erased as soon as all the cars bunched up behind one another. While track marshals were busy craning away Grosjean's Lotus and collecting debris at turn 14, remaining cars weaved through the circuit at a regulated speed, keeping the tyres warmed; standard procedure during a safety period.

"Okay Kimi, we need to keep working all four tyres please! Keep working all four tyres..." Slade back on the radio, reminding him of the importance of keeping the tyres at optimal level for racing conditions.

"Yes yes yes yes, I am doing it all the time, you don't have to remind me every 10 seconds!" Räikkönen reminded him who was the driver, again.

Race engineers are paid to relay information to drivers during the course of a typical Grand Prix weekend; that includes all three sessions of the practice runs, qualifying session and the all-important race. They are obligated to do so regardless of the response from the driver. They are remunerated to make sure the drivers have everything at their fingertips to cross the chequered flag in the best possible position. These may include coaching, telling the driver to adjust certain settings on their steering wheels for better performance, or conditioning the machines. This was banned temporarily, as some believe Formula One drivers had lost the edge in pure racing, whilst relying too much on technical input from the team. It was obvious the Finn did not need any advice from his engineer or the team, he just wanted to be able to put his head down and set purple sectors that were quick enough to be ahead for the rest of the race.

He did just that. Räikkönen soaked up the pressure, having Alonso in his gearbox in the closing stages of the race. He eventually crossed the line 0.852 seconds before his former teammate Alonso. The margin was not something that would bother him, or anyone in the Lotus team for that matter, as long as he was the first to cross. It was a sweet victory with his new team and cemented his driving for the rest of us. Not that it would matter to him, because trust me, you and I would be the last person he would want to impress.

This is Kimi Räikkönen. The man who cares only about racing when he is behind the wheels. The man I came to love this sport with.

Life Lesson #6
Be Like Kimi

Before the 2012 Abu Dhabi Grand Prix, Räikkönen was known for his could-not-care-less personality in the paddock; he is a fan favourite because of his persona on and off the track. His short and direct responses at press conferences, and his cool demeanour on the circuit, make him one of a kind. On the grid, drivers are categorised by various characteristics and, for the sake of stereotyping, Formula One drivers are perceived as flamboyant, fiery, arrogant, vocal, utterly uncompromising, charismatic, playboyish etc. However, with modern Formula One filled with politics, protocols and marketing guidelines, the drivers are well marketed to portray their image to align their teams' branding and sponsorship commitments. Teams treat their drivers as their number one asset. They are well-drilled, by all means, to look after their image, and they speak in a sanitised language that is scripted by their PR team to satisfy today's needy press. In other words, drivers use cut and paste answers to fulfil their media duties. With relentless scrutiny with everything in Formula One, drivers today are trained to present themselves just like a pop culture icon; to act and say the right thing, to be politically correct and apologetic if not.

> *"Being an F1 driver is a crazy job but not what everyone expects. My year consists of 20% driving and 80% media, marketing, and travel."*
>
> Daniel Ricciardo

PR activities, including the official press conference, media interviews, and sponsor commitments, are the least of Raikkonen's concerns during a Formula One season. His focus is solely on racing and any additional baggage is considered a nuisance to him. However, all drivers are contracted by Formula One to attend press conferences and interviews throughout race weekends. For Räikkönen, he made it clear to the public that he had little interest in that part of the game. Räikkönen's no-nonsense, monotonal and disinterested approach makes him a rare species on the grid.

In one of the interviews, he was asked about what gets him going during a typical race weekend.

"The most exciting moments during the race weekend?" asked the interviewer.

"I think it's the race start, always." Räikkönen answered.

"The most boring?" continued by the interviewer.

"Now." the Finn responded with his sheer bluntness.

On another occasion, he was asked about the brand he was endorsing during the years he was with McLaren.

"What makes TAG Heuer so special?"

"It's Okay." he replied, with his typical short answer.

And in the post-race interview at the Abu Dhabi Grand Prix, ex-Formula One driver, David Coulthard asked him some after-race thoughts.

"Kimi, your first victory since the 2009 Belgian Grand Prix. Tell us about your emotions at this time."

"Not much really." he answered.

Rest assured, Räikkönen does not sugarcoat.

"Formula One would be a paradise without the media."

Kimi Räikkönen

Keeping a Cool Head

The Finn's nickname "Iceman", given by his former boss Ron Dennis during his tenure at McLaren, says more about his driving than his origins. He certainly does not fit into the category of hot-headed drivers. We used to see much footage from the past on drivers' furious brawls after an on-track crash. Drivers going at each other's throats, words spat and punches thrown in anger. Or in more contemporary settings, with more civilised acts, drivers throwing tantrums by smashing their $100,000.00 highly sophisticated steering wheels onto the ground. At times, I can understand the frustration they were going through, whether it was an accident with no fault of their own or a malfunction to hardware that forced the car to a halt. Whatever it was, it was so costly for the drivers to bear that they needed to take it out on someone or something. After all, what is lost could be a race win, podium, or championship points that could count towards their campaign and prize money for the weekend. Not so applicable for Räikkönen though. He typically would take it with a grain of salt; not that he does not care, but he knew there was nothing else he could have done. So he chose to move on.

In 2008, when Räikkönen was at the peak of his career, he was set to defend his world title with Scuderia Ferrari. During the Canadian Grand Prix, race leaders Hamilton, Kubica and Räikkönen all dived down the pit lane during the safety car period; Ferrari's swift pit work allowed Räikkönen to be dispatched before his rivals. Before exiting the pit lane, Räikkönen stopped at the end of the pit lane as the red light was indicating the pit lane was closed, hence no cars were allowed to be released back onto the track. As most teams and drivers were panicking and trying to take advantage of the safety car intervention, Räikkönen stayed cool and calm and spotted the red light. He stopped the car, together with Kubica next to him. Hamilton had a brain fart, and went right into the back of the defending champion's F2008, creating a chain reaction with Hamilton's karting mate Nico Rosberg hitting the back of Hamilton's McLaren. Räikkönen and Hamilton retired immediately with the terminal damage, Rosberg and Kubica continued their race. As both Räikkönen and Hamilton walked towards their garage, Räikkönen patted Hamilton and pointed him to the lights to tell him about his mistake. He then walked past the Brits and moved on. No fights, no argument, no dispute, no nonsense. It was not his fault he had lost a potential race win, but he quickly moved on.

On a separate occasion in the 2006 Monaco Grand Prix, the year when the Finn was still driving for McLaren, the younger Räikkönen was coming off one of his best seasons, winning seven races in the previous year and finishing runner up behind Alonso in the championship. During the race at Monte Carlo, coincidentally, it was also during a safety car period that saw Räikkönen's race come to an early termination while he was holding P2. His MP4-21, suffering from unreliability throughout the season, was toasting in this incident, forcing Räikkönen to stop at the turn of Portier to escape from the fire. Again, his race was over through no fault of his own. He lived with it and moved on; removing himself out of the cockpit safely was his priority. He did just that and walked away from his disappointment. The only problem at the time was, he had a long walk in front of him to his pit garage. The camera managed to capture him walking alongside the track and inside the famous tunnel of the Monaco circuit. While the race was happening in the background, the TV director showed a strong interest in Räikkönen's excursion. The Finn did not return to the pit garage to have words with his team, engineers or mechanics. He did not think it was imperative, since he was no longer in the race. Instead, he returned to his private yacht that happened to be docked alongside the port. No whinging, no tantrum, no meltdown, no nonsense. It was not his fault he lost a potential podium finish, but he quickly moved on.

In 2009, Räikkönen stepped up to the plate to show his coolness once again in front of the global audience, and I was lucky to be on-site to witness it. The 2009 Malaysian Grand Prix was remembered for its downpour that halted the race midway. The race was red-flagged when rain was bucketing down, while drivers were left hanging to find out their fate that stormy afternoon. Monsoon rain with lightning strikes flooded the 5.6km track. Cars left on the grid, with mechanics scrambling around. Some drivers stayed in their cockpits, others taking a spell trackside. Where I was, I had a good view of the big screen right next to turn 1. The fans, like myself, at the circuit, were left to wait for the rain to subside before any chance to see the race resume before the 2-hour race[5] time expired. All we had was the big screen to keep us entertained for the time being. The camera captured Webber, the director of GPDA[6], the Formula One drivers' union, running up and down the grid to get a word from his fellow drivers regarding their thoughts on continuing the race. 30 minutes passed and the rain did not seem to back down; the likelihood of a restart was slim. Assessing the situation, perhaps Räikkönen knew in advance. While other drivers were still loitering around the grid, Räikkönen was already in his khaki shorts, his racing suit was long gone, he was captured on the big screen eating what looked to be a Magnum chocolate ice cream while taking a bottle of coke from the fridge to reinvigorate himself with some post-race snacks. The race eventually ended as it was, Räikkönen's car was way out of points, nothing was there for him to gain, so he showed us once again he was as cool as a cucumber, and had quickly moved on.

These are all classic Kimi Räikkönen's footage you can easily google online. They say a lot about his character as a racing driver. Calm, cool, collected, composed, centred when he is behind the wheel, chilled with no-frills when his crash helmet and gloves are off. No grey areas and you never have to read between the lines with Räikkönen. He is WYSIWYG; what you see is what you get. Apolitical, as he gets on with all his teammates throughout his career. Well, he just could not care less about what others were up to. He took care of business and let the race result do all the talking. He is the true jewel of Formula One.

In life, we want to stay calm to make good decisions. Unlike Formula One drivers behind the wheel, we do not necessarily need to make split second decisions, nevertheless, staying calm allows our brains to work and think straight. This is utterly important when it comes to confronting great stress, working under the pump. In this fast-paced world, we are constantly trying

5 Formula One race is capped at 2-hour limit, this excludes the time if the race was red-flagged for track incident or weather condition. The race must conclude upon the 2-hour limit.

6 GPDA is the Grand Prix Drivers' Association, formed in 1961 to take care of affairs in the best interest of the drivers.

to keep up the pace on a day to day basis. It is the norm for us to react and respond to a question, a problem, an issue without further delay.

"Focusing on one thing and doing it really, really well can get you very far."
Kevin Systrom

In the meantime, we also want to focus on the things that matter. Räikkönen only cares about racing, nothing more. He would give everything to the race, but once he left his cockpit, and took off his crash helmet, he no longer needed to think about racing, being very clear-cut with work and everything else. He was paid to race and all his focus will always be on the track. Everything away from the track, the interviews and all, though part of his job description contract, had absolutely no impact on his performance on the track, therefore needed minimal attention from him. I admire him for that. Focusing on the things that matter, and making sure we have given it our all; everything after that is not something you and I should be concerned or even worried about. During a day at the office, we work hard and dedicate a solid eight hours, or however long it may be, with all our might, then leave the workplace with nothing but ourselves; work is not supposed to accompany us to our next destination, wherever it may be. It should stop when we clock off and all work should be left behind.

Räikkönen is my hero in many ways and, when I titled this life lesson "Be like Kimi", it was not meant to be all literal. Yes, his calm and cool demeanour is something worth mirroring, however, what I had in mind, was more so to be like Kimi with regard to how he is only trying to be like himself. In life, we often lose our identity as to who we are and who we want to be based on pressure from parents, peers, society and the world at large. To be a good son and daughter to our parents; a diligent student to our teachers; a responsible parent to our children; a faithful partner to our spouse; a noble citizen to our country. Whatever or to whoever it may be, there are a lot of identities to be filled and met. Having fulfilled all these roles, are we still who we want to be?

"Let go of who you think you're supposed to be; embrace who you are."
Brene Brown

It is not always an easy answer, and some people take a lifetime to discover their true self. I may not be able to offer much but, perhaps by a process of elimination, we can at least start by finding out who we are not. Rolf Dobelli in his book "Questions to Ask of Life" may be able to provide some thought-provoking questions about who we are (or not) and what we stand for. Dobelli poses questions to life in the most profound and unexpected way, taking a different lens to delve into love, marriage, morals, conscience, politics, identity, friendship, education, success, career, age, death, God and many more. I spend a good time reading and finding my answers to questions that correlate to my core values. The book is written in German and only translated and published in Azerbaijani, Chinese, Greek and Korean. Here are some interesting questions that I attempted to translate them from the Chinese version that are worth asking ourselves:

"If you still are a piece of blank paper, who should be writing on it, is it you or someone else?"

"How efficient are you at pursuing life goals that are not suitable for you?"

"Hypothetically speaking, if you can 'pre-live' your life, would you still choose to be born?"

"Do you often take on roles that were not appreciated?"

"How does someone's upbringing/education reflect in a war?"

"What is worst, how people think about you or how people talk about you?"

The Inner Child

Dobelli's questions helped me to confront my core values through a rather interesting perspective. Correction, perspectives. To extend this exercise to place a lens from inside out rather than the other way around. Finding your inner child that has been undermined and liberating the child inside to embrace authenticity. Pablo Picasso, arguably one of the most influential artists of the modernism movement, was known for pioneering Cubism in the 20th century. The industrial revolution had changed the landscape of the world and transitioned to modernity, while every artist took a shot at taking a different lens to express what art was or would be in that context. Picasso had an illustrative career and had different phases of his life, documenting various styles of painting from blue period through to formulation of cubism. Undoubtedly he was talented with exceptional skills, yet he was always trying to discover, or rather uncover, his ability to paint like a child. His famous quote, *"It took me four years to paint like Raphael, but a lifetime to paint like a child"* explained his desire to be able to express his art in the rawest form. This idea provokes how we mature into adulthood with expectations and guidelines whilst often neglect our creative ability, based on the soul of the child we once were.

> *"All children are artists. The problem is how to remain an artist once he grows up."*
>
> Pablo Picasso

Too often in life, we allow others to dictate who we are, tempted to compare ourselves with someone else. The someone-else may have overwhelmed us with their qualities and attributes, leading us to feel demoralised in our journey. The universal truth is, we are incomparable individuals. American neo soul singer Jill Scott encourages everyone to be themselves. When asked about performing after fellow singer Erykah Badu, she nailed it with this, *"We all have our own thing and that's the magic, but everybody comes with their own sense of strength and their own queendom. Mine could never compare to hers and hers could never compare to mine."*

"Your biggest rival is the one in your mirror."
Rolf Dobelli

As ironic as it sounds, this lesson teaches me to be like Kimi in how he is doing his best to be himself. This is a lesson not asking anyone to be like Kimi, but to be like ourselves. Paradoxically, this is just like parenting. How many times have we heard parents asking their children to be obedient, follow rules and do not try anything silly; at the same time they urge them to step outside the boundaries and explore the world. To play by the rules but also to break some to be creative. Ironic as it sounds, and I am not going to lie, it is something for us to find out. Are we being authentic or are we being who someone else had in mind? These are questions worth asking ourselves. Life is about self-discovery, what rules to keep and what boundaries to challenge; we might not know what we want or who we want to be, depending on the route we take. Whatever our status may be on this road of discovery, just a gentle reminder to ask ourselves an awful lot of questions.

Otherwise, take my advice and take a chill pill, keep calm and focus and be like Kimi.

"I never do anything to please anyone."
Kimi Räikkönen

FUN FACTS ON KIMI RÄIKKÖNEN

Kimi Räikkönen is the most senior driver on the grid in 2020 season, with 315 races under his belt. He is one of three world champions Finland has produced, the other two are Keke Rosberg and Mika Häkkinen. The Finn is the only driver to arrive at Formula One without F3, GP2 or F2 experience. He has the record of the fastest laps (10) in a single season in 2004, 2005 and 2008. Ironically, those years were not fruitful in terms of his championship aspirations. The Iceman is also known as The King of Spa, having won four times at Spa-Francorchamps, Belgium. He is the only driver to win races with V10, V8 and hybrid V6 engines in the history of Formula One, showing his dominance and adaptability to win across three generations of engines. The oldest statesman in Formula One remains the last Ferrari world champion as of 2020 and one of three Ferrari world champions since 1979; the other two are Michael Schumacher and Jody Scheckter. As of 2020, he has raced the most kilometres of any driver, with the most races finished and most podiums (30) in different circuits. Räikkönen is indeed a living part of Formula One history.

WATCH

2003 Malaysian Grand Prix, 2012 Abu Dhabi Grand Prix, 2018 United States Grand Prix.

DID YOU KNOW

Kimi Räikkönen almost drove the Lotus F1 team to bankruptcy? During his two-year tenure with the team, he had overachieved his contract goals and Lotus could not, and did not, pay him his remuneration and bonuses in full.

Turn 3

Senna S

Autódromo José Carlos Pace

-23.700870619292118, -46.69796513162175

RACE 7

2012 Brazilian Grand Prix

71 Laps

"Use the best of your talent,
we know how big it is, use it..."

The Last Dance

If you did not skip the last two chapters, and I truly hope that is the case, then you would be expecting this. The fitting closure for season 2012.

2012 was to be remembered as one of the finest seasons in Formula One history. It is unquestionably at the top of my list when it comes to ranking the best season in my young Formula One journey. The travelling circus took on 20 cities across five continents, the most races covered within seven months. Six world champions on the grid trying to add one more accolade to their trophy collection against 18 other drivers who were eyeing their first crack at the title. 12 teams fighting for the FIA World Constructors' Championship, the ultimate team glory, and prize money to build their next campaign. The season produced eight different race winners, unprecedentedly, seven different victors from the first seven races. Fittingly, the drivers' championship was neck and neck to the final race. It would only make sense to bid farewell to the season with a finale that had a good track record for a title decider.

The pilgrimage to the ultimate glory. Destination: Sao Paulo, Brazil. Checked.

There has been a handful of title deciders hosted by Brazil in the recent history. 2004 and 2005 when a young Fernando Alonso was crowned double world champion in his Renault over Kimi Räikkönen and Michael Schumacher respectively. 2009 saw a dream fairy tale for Jenson Button when he secured his only title with Brawn GP at Interlagos[1]. These were all good solid races, do not get me wrong, but these title deciders were incomparable to the theatrical endings of 2007 and 2008. These two year's finales, let's just say, were not for the faint-hearted.

2007, the three-way title fight between Alonso, Lewis Hamilton and Räikkönen was highly anticipated with drama when Hamilton mysteriously lost his gears to drop back to the field and allow Räikkönen to claim race victory, and the world title by a single point in an epic narrative. Räikkönen had a 17-point[2] deficit with two races remaining and a tall mountain to climb, yet everything turned in his favour at the right moment. The Finn's sole driver's championship, to date, also happens to be Ferrari's last.

The following year saw Ferrari's Felipe Massa, seemingly following in the footsteps of Räikkönen, as second driver to win the drivers' title for the Italian team for the second successive year. We all thought for a moment, or for 38 seconds when he crossed the line to the chequered flag claiming race victory on home soil, a perfect ending and dream fairy tale at its best. Nothing beats the feeling of winning a world title at home, in a neighbourhood where he grew up watching races over the fence. That dream was short-lived, sorry to break it to you. It was destined to be denied by Hamilton 38 seconds later, a late passing of Timo Glock's Toyota in the rain, gaining the extra points that elevated the Brit to be the world champion by a single point. It happened on the last corner of the

1 Interlagos is the neighbourhood located in the district of Socorro in the city of São Paulo, pundits often refer the circuit as Interlagos instead of official name of Autódromo José Carlos Pace.

2 Championship points in season 2007 were awarded to the top 8 drivers only. With the distribution of 10, 8, 6, 5, 4, 3, 2, 1.

final race of the season. That was what we call in basketball, hitting the game-winning buzzer-beater. It was heartbreaking for the nation and gut-wrenching, particularly if your surname spelt Massa. For Hamilton, that was the redemption for which he was desperate, and it was make or break for his career. It later proved he had turned the corner, pun intended, and he had steered himself to six world titles by 2019.

Track condition: wet and forecast rain. Checked.

The great equaliser, how can I forget that. The best shows up in the rain. It was more fitting that he did so in the title decider, the season finale. The wet conditions meant a lot more thinking and mind games between drivers and teams. Who was going to show their hand first, and make the right call under the pump? I always have the impression that Formula One teams employ some of the most intelligent and creative individuals, and must have all the strategies in place and know all the plans from A to B to C. But, let the truth be told, I have seen teams getting the wrong calls on strategies from time to time, even from the big players, the big teams. Every driver or every team to me is vulnerable in this element of the race. The rain plays a big factor and every single detail could be the difference between heaven or earth.

The context: two double world champions going for their third. Checked.

After 19 races, the two title contenders had emerged from the pool of the 24 elite drivers. Fernando Alonso of the Scuderia Ferrari versus Sebastian Vettel of the Red Bull Racing. The oldest motorsport giant from Italy versus the new up and coming party-driven energy drink brand from Austria. In the historical context, it may seem like a classic David versus Goliath narrative, but odds on paper said otherwise. The Spanish versus the German; both double world champions at the time, chasing the elusive third drivers' title. Alonso had led the championship for most of the season, shouldering an average challenger of his F2012 and securing three race wins in 19 tries. It was evident Alonso was not equipped with the fastest machine, only putting his name on pole twice while championship rival Vettel recorded five race wins to his tally, with five pole positions prior to the season finale. They were 13 points apart heading into this race. The scenarios were; Vettel needed to finish in the top four to win regardless of where Alonso finished. Alonso, on the other hand, needed at least a podium finish and hoped for Vettel to finish no higher than P5.

The punters were putting their money on Alonso to pull out some bunnies from his hat, just like he had done throughout the season, pushing his car to the limit and simply overachieving his way to contest for the title on the last Sunday of the season. The odds were against the Spaniard, though. Despite previously claiming his first two titles here at Sao Paulo, his qualifying position this time around did not sit well with the bookies. Vettel put his RB8 on P4, while Alonso was a couple of rows behind at P7. The German just needed to finish where he started to get the job done, hence was a clear favourite in this title fight. All eyes were on the pair, and paid little attention to the front row where it was a McLaren lockout with Hamilton and Button.

Sunday, 20th of November, just a month away from Christmas, the showdown was about to get underway at the Autódromo José Carlos Pace, the track named after the native Formula One legend who won the 1975 Brazilian Grand Prix. Whose Christmas would come early? We were all eager to find out as the clock ticked to the race start. I was one of the seven million who tuned in to the race, sitting alone in my living room in the middle of the night, all geared up with drinks and supper. My TV network brought live coverage from the other side of the world, and the first image I could see was the raindrops on the camera lens. The God of Formula One had spoken and requested a fair race under the rain. I pushed myself closer to my TV with high anticipation. *'May the best man win'*, I said to myself.

The formation lap kicked off for one last time in 2012, the final time for the great Michael Schumacher, the seven-time world champion saying goodbye to the fans for the second and final time. Coincidentally, Schumacher also had his final race before his first retirement at the same circuit in the 2006 version of the Brazil Grand Prix. The affair six years prior had a different hype around him, as he was entering his title showdown with Alonso, whilst in 2012, Schumacher's Grand Prix entry was merely a sideshow. This was also the final time for the pole sitter Hamilton, suiting up for McLaren before moving to Mercedes for 2013 and beyond. The Brit's 110th race entry, aiming to finish his tenure with McLaren on a good note, hoping to bid for another victory for the team that had nurtured him since he was 14.

The cars left the grid to commence their formation lap, weaving to generate heat and grip on the 4.3km anticlockwise track whilst a sea of mechanics, team personnel, media and camera crew rushed across the pit straight in chaos to find their garage and spots, to ready themselves for the start before the cars made their way back. The top 10 drivers lined up into their grid slots in order. The two British drivers for McLaren locked out the front row with Hamilton taking pole and Button starting alongside. The next row belonged to the two Red Bulls, with Aussie Mark Webber edging out his German teammate slash title contender Vettel in P3 and P4 respectively followed by Felipe Massa of Ferrari, Nico Hülkenberg of Force India, and the second title contender in Alonso with Räikkönen of Lotus rounding off the top eight.

Let the fight begin.

Lights out. Wheels spun and cars flew towards the first corner under a light misty rain. The rain was not visible for the moment, hence all cars were fitted with slicks. The drivers powered their cars uphill ready for the left-hander then right, known as the Senna S, the corner named after the Brazilian legend, the late Ayrton Senna. The two McLarens had a decent getaway, but not the Red Bulls. Both Webber and Vettel struggled to awake their tardy bulls, allowing Massa and Alonso to go around from outside entering turn 1. Massa was quick to make his move with late braking and leapfrogged one of the McLarens to snatch P2 after just two corners into the race. Massa's teammate Alonso was equally impressive with his start, and overtook several cars and found himself in P4 before turn 3.

Where was Vettel? The German had a handful, dealing with cars that caged him through the first two turns and dropped him down from P4 to P7. In the space of two corners, Vettel and Alonso had swapped their position on the track. If you thought that was not enough to begin the title decider with, here comes more.

The championship leader Vettel approached turn 4, a sharp left-hander, and turned into Bruno Senna's Williams, clipped and spun and subsequently took out Pérez on the way. Debris was flying, big pieces coming off cars, possibly front or rear wings, but was not entirely sure from whom. Vettel and his partner in crime, Abbey, was a rabbit in the headlights, facing the wrong way on the track and seeing all his competitions streaking past. We knew his car had sustained damage but we, like Vettel inside his cockpit, needed to wait precious seconds for all the cars to get by him before he could find out his fate for the race and his championship hope. Those seconds seemed eternal for him. Eventually, Abbey turned and made a dramatic spin and finally pointed herself in the right direction, and off she went again. He was P20 with Senna and Pérez becoming the first two casualties for the race from that incident, while Vettel had found himself under the perfect storm.

Wow! In the space of 30 seconds, the tables had turned. Alonso now had the upper hand when his rival had thrown away the advantage of his track position. Merely 30 seconds ago, Vettel's mission was to have a clean race and finish where he started. Now, he was not even sure if his car was

healthy enough to continue, and for how long, let alone climbing back
up the order. The Red Bull team were concerned, and they had every
the reasons to be. The championship was at stake, and with their backs
against the wall, they asked Vettel to stay in the race while they studied
the condition of the car. Adrian Newey, their chief designer, the technical
guru behind so many championship-winning cars in the last three decades,
obtained a photo that was taken by their team and pretty much had his
work cut out. From our TV screens, one of the many 250 onsite cameras
had tried to capture Vettel's car in slow motion playback, and it clearly
showed some seriously damaged sidepod[3] on the left of the bodywork.

Red Bull gives you wings, the famous slogan for the Austrian energy-
boosting drink, ironically, this was something Vettel was hoping to have.
The German needed a boost after positioning himself at the worst
possible scenario, nursing his RB7 with bruised feathers. Whatever
damage was there, Vettel needed his car to hold it together for 70 more
laps. The defending champion had been thrown into the deep end when
the race had not even completed its first lap. While Vettel was catching
the pack, the front runners were coming around the last corner and
heading for the main straight to complete the first lap of the race. The
two McLarens were ahead; the battle lay between Webber, Massa and
Alonso. Massa was closing in on Webber, picking up a tow[4] and fancied
his chances coming out to his right. Surprisingly, Alonso pulled out a move
of his own, being the last car in the trio, dived down the inside into turn
1 and overtook both Massa and Webber in one single move. That moved
him up into P3, the podium finish he needed to win this championship; a
crucial position to obtain at the early stage of the race. Bear in mind, at
this time, only 5 cars have completed their first lap, with 70 more to go to
conclude the season.

---

3 Sidepod is the part of the car that flanks the sides of the monocoque alongside the driver and
runs back to the rear wing, housing the radiators.

4 Tow also known as slipstream is a driving tactic when a driver can to catch the car ahead and
duck in behind its rear wing to benefit from a reduction in drag and hopefully be able to achieve
a superior maximum speed to slingshot past before the next corner.

Alonso had steered himself into the position he needed to be; the rest lay with his rival. Where Vettel finishes will determine the fate of both drivers. Just as I thought, Alonso's flying start was impressive, his left front locked up and went wide into turn 1 on lap 5 with the track becoming increasingly damp. The short excursion dropped him behind the surprising Hülkenberg of Force India. Meanwhile, Vettel was determined by the speed he was showing, setting the fastest lap and making up places lap by lap, surging up to P6 by lap 9, and just one position between the two championship rivals by lap 17. Nothing Alonso could do.

The rain intensified, Vettel and Alonso both pitted for wet tyres to cover each other off, the move proved to be questionable as the rain quickly ceased. The two race leaders at the time, Button and Hülkenberg extended their lead over the others, as they did not make any pit stops. Red Bull had been dominant all year with speed, acing corners all season long, but that day, Vettel's Abbey was on another level, she was bulletproof. She kept Alonso honest by pacing herself behind the red car. Nothing Alonso could do. Not as if he could deliberately take Vettel out like they used to do in the 80s or 90s. Alonso was down on points, so he needed to outscore Vettel by a set margin, and his current position just wouldn't cut it. It felt like Vettel had made up his handicap in just 20 laps, and we were pretty much back to where it all began.

There were many dramas in between. The erratic rain made it all extremely difficult to follow in terms of team strategies. The safety car was out to settle the cars. The restart saw Kobayashi, then Massa subsequently passing Vettel, as his damaged Red Bull was significantly slow on a drying track. Alonso at P4 while Vettel, demoted a few places back at P7, still had enough to bag the title. Hülkenberg was leading the race for a duration, which gave the Force India staff some butterflies in their tummies. Hamilton took the lead when Hülkenberg spun his car but soon after the Force India driver, the anxious and ambitious German, crashed into

Hamilton and took out the Brit for good. His compatriot Button inherited the lead while promoting Alonso to P2. The drama continued when Vettel's radio died and all team communication was limited to old-fashioned pit board.

"The difference in winning and losing is, most often not quitting."
Walt Disney

As the race approached the last 5 laps, Alonso at P2 and Vettel at P5 would see the German winning the drivers' title. It then reminded me of the radio message from two years prior when Alonso was fighting for his title in Abu Dhabi, the season finale in 2010.

"Use the best of your talent, we know how big it is, use it…" the Ferrari race engineer trying to rally Alonso to dig deeper in his Italian accent.

Alonso could not pull the bunny out of the hat under the lights in one of the richest soil in the Middle East at the beginning of the new decade; he could not do more either in Interlagos two years later. No miracles then, no miracles now for the Spaniard. No last corner heroic moves as he was too far away from the race leader Button. In fact, the race or the season had to end prematurely when the safety car was deployed for Paul Di Resta's accident. With just one lap to go, all cars had to stay in their current positions and cross the chequered flag as they were. Hence, almost guaranteeing Vettel's third title, unless Button suffers a mechanical failure and bumps Alonso into P1. But no. No miracle for Alonso, unfortunately. He crossed the line P2 and Vettel at P4, and the triple world champion was born.

"Sebastian, you are a triple world champion!" Christian Horner congratulated his driver on the radio.

Life Lesson #7
Life is Unfair

Alonso missed out on the championship by a mere three points; it was not meant to be, for the third time in six years. Yes, I was rooting for Alonso, backing the underdog. An underdog narrative was far more inspiring. After all, 2012 was the year that Linsanity[5] made headlines in New York and turned into a global sensation. And especially with the Red Bull dominance from the previous two years, it was enough for me to believe dethroning the defending champion was the best script for Formula One at the time. Despite my favouritism, Vettel deserved the championship. After all, he had proved to be invincible, even after his car seemed unfit to endure the afternoon. Driving a compromised machine, it was a colossal effort to mount such a challenge on the biggest day of the year. He was indeed a worthy champion. As for Alonso, I felt for him for his agonising defeat. The cameras captured both drivers after leaving their cockpit. Alonso was looking despairing under his crash helmet; he could not have done more with his relentless pursuit of greatness. He was bordering on superhuman and had extracted every bit from his car in every race, yet he fell short by a few points, once again. In a season where he fought tooth and nail with Vettel, Alonso without a shadow of doubt was the most complete driver on the grid. However, his calibre did not translate to the final standing. And the cruel reality is that there is no consolation coming second. The best driver for the year was not awarded with the ultimate glory, and for a moment in my head, the outcome did not seem just, and in my heart, I was crying out *"it's so unfair"*.

Well, life is unfair...sometimes. As much as we want to believe we deserve to win, we won't always come out as victors, be it the promotion we worked so hard for, or the contract on which we tried to bid. Reality is, we can all

5 Linsanity was term coined during the sudden rise of Jeremy Lin (then of the NBA's New York Knicks) to basketball stardom in 2012.

be diligently working our way to be the best of ourselves, but that does not warrant the outcome for which we hoped or desired. Sometimes luck comes into play, and other times it is just not meant to be. When it does happen that way, we all need to learn to take it with a grain of salt, because the simple fact is, but perhaps the hardest lesson to understand, is that life is unfair. Far from being cynical, that is how the way life works. Or perhaps it is only true that life is not fair for everyone, making it fair for all.

> *"Life is not fair, never was, it isn't now and it won't ever be."*
> Matthew McConaughey

There are similarities in how Formula One works for the team or the driver to how life works for people. Formula One was not established based on fair or equal terms. The fact that there are no strict rules to refrain teams from spending or investing in design and manufacturing the fastest car in the world, the big boys will always get a head start in this sport. The likes of Ferrari and Mercedes have enormous budgets and substantially more dollars to spend on their R&D, wind tunnels[6], hiring high profile staff and courting top drivers. These unfair advantages against medium and smaller teams are nothing new in the world of Formula One.

The Ferrari Rule

The inequitable game lies in the payout. Teams get paid by Formula One based on a few guidelines. Apart from the obvious prize money from winning races during the season and classification fees for entering and staying in the competition, there are a few unfair or unspoken rules. There is bonus money for constructors' championship awarded to the top teams, making the big teams stay bigger. Some teams may be eligible for a special payment, for instance, Williams was granted a "heritage payment"

---

6 Wind tunnel is a room built to test airflow and analyse the aerodynamics of the car and parts the team designed and built. A 1:2 scale model is built for a wind tunnel test.

during 2017 of $10 million. Other teams may be subject to other bonus payments if they meet certain targets or special requirements previously agreed by Formula One. The most controversial of all would be a payment called "Long-Standing Team"; a bonus payment in recognition of their "historical franchise"; In this case, Scuderia Ferrari, the oldest team from Italy that have raced in every season since 1950, are awarded an annual payment of a whopping $68 million.

When Mercedes finished their season as constructor champions in 2016, they were paid a total of $171 million, including all the bonuses. Finishing third in the constructors' championship was Ferrari, and the team from Maranello made $180 million with the aid of this special payment. Clearly, the prancing horse got the lion's share and that itself does not sound like fair play in my book. Ferrari was at the top of the pay chart with $180 million, in comparison to $19 million received by HASS, a relatively new team in 2016; a gap of $161 million between the two teams did little to encourage the newcomers to be competitive on the track. That does not in any shape or form help the teams to be at the same level on the playing field.

> ## "...a sport is supposed to be fair and Formula 1 is not fair."
> ### Romain Grosjean

This difference in financial standing leads to discrepancies in human resources. HASS employed approximately 200 staff to run their team, whilst Red Bull had the capacity of more than 800 talents in 22 departments working for the Milton Keynes based group. The big boys like Ferrari and Mercedes have the manpower of over 1,000 staff in their Formula One vicinity. This, however, does not stop teams from entering or leaving in the competition. Survival of the fittest is a centuries-old principle that is never out of date, the rich snowball and the poor struggle.

Capitalism, commercialism, politics and red tape all contribute to the fact that we are living in a competitive world; that is what it is.

Parenting in an Unfair World

I have two daughters and I often find myself in the conundrum of splitting equal time and love to them both. As hard as it sounds, it is virtually impossible to achieve even-stevens with them every time. My rationale is that I want them to feel equally loved and foster in them an understanding of the principle of fairness. As they grew older, I often heard them complaining, *"that's not fair"* and the frequency grew by days. I have since stopped teaching my daughters about expecting fairness in life, whether it is from me, my wife or from sources outside our home. On the contrary, I promote the motto of *"life isn't fair"* to prepare them for the realm of the outside world. Acknowledging this does not mean I am teaching them to succumb to defeat in life; it only means they ought to face challenges and adversities from unbalanced situations. These may happen to them more often than others, and that could only mean they are getting more opportunities to prove their worthiness in life. Life is unfair and it always was, and the sooner they learn that, the better.

One of the reasons to explain our desire, or my daughters', to seek justice or fairness in life is based on the effect called 'just-world' fallacy; it is a cognitive bias that causes people to make direct relation to one's actions towards fitting consequences. The common ideology of "you reap what you sow". Getting rewarded when we do good and punished for evil deeds is also sometimes referred to as karma. It is a fallacy for obvious reasons that the world cannot be just, as we cannot control events in our lives to meet these criteria. The reason we practice just-world fallacy unconsciously is because it serves as a motivation to push us toward our goals, believing hard work pays dividends; it makes us feel in control when we expect an equal outcome from our relative output.

"Life isn't fair.
We need to educate a younger generation."
Bernie Ecclestone

Grass is Greener

In life, we get so caught up with the things that are happening over our fences; whether our neighbour's grass is greener or healthier. "The Neighbour's Window", a 2020 Academy Award winner for a short film took on a lens to look at a mother of two young children, Alli, and her life as a mother struggling with daily rigour and her mundane life with her husband. One day, through their apartment window, Alli and her husband unwittingly notice a younger couple who lived across their street. They watched the couple and began to desire their lifestyles and relationship, a reflection of their younger selves, living freely without children. Following their neighbour's day-to-day life through their window became a ritual, so did their envious feelings. Until one day, Alli found out the young couple was facing some health issues of their own and, not long after, the husband of the young couple passed away. Alli approached the young widow to offer her condolences, only to find out that the widow herself had been watching Alli and her family all this time. The widow and her late husband were doing exactly what Alli and her husband were doing; envying their neighbour's life.

We become vulnerable when we start to peek over the fence and make comparisons between lifestyles. Envy is the culprit of this "life isn't fair" sentiment, or the common root cause. We pay attention to others despite the fact that, whether life over the fence is better or worse, has got nothing to do with us and the level of our happiness in life. Again, as mentioned in Chapter 2, focusing illusion can and will misdirect us to wrong places for the wrong reasons. Focus on ourselves and our lawn; if they are not green enough to our liking, work on it!

"Don't compare your life to others. There's no comparison between the sun and the moon. They shine when it's their time."

Cassey Ho

The feisty charge from Vettel made the tightly choreographed race exhilarating and kept me on the edge of my seat all night long. The 2012 Brazilian Grand Prix was Alonso's last bid at the drivers' title. With all the tribulation he endured, he took the defeat and kept his chin high, crediting his team and his rival. In all honesty, he made Ferrari relevant again in that three-year stretch, and a genuine threat to the Red Bulls. Nevertheless, he never recovered in terms of finding the right situation and with the right team thereafter, making several questionable off-track decisions which lead him to exit the sport by 2018, on a low with the struggling McLaren team. After missing his boat, his fighting spirit stayed hopeful, finding his way back to the sport by putting himself in prime position for a comeback while competing in the likes of IndyCar series and LeMans. Still chasing the elusive dream, the ultimate motorsport glory of the Triple Crown with triumph in Indianapolis 500, Monaco Grand Prix and 24 Hours LeMans, with the latter two he had achieved twice in 2007/08 and 2018/19.

Success is never a guarantee in Formula One, neither is it in life. We are not always expected to win or perform at a peak level with the situation that surrounds us. Alonso acknowledged his success with gratitude, *"It is true - maybe with five or seven points more, I could be five times world champion. But on the other hand, I could have zero world championships, and zero wins or zero podiums, because F1 is an extremely competitive environment. So I just take the positives, and I am happy with my achievements."* Success is not guaranteed by the amount of effort or hard work. What is more important is to keep our spirits high, reserve our winning mentality and fight for more wins in different aspects of our life. Life is short, do not cry over spilt milk or argue with life, as it owes us nothing. Life is only fair when it's never fair for everyone.

> *"Only one guy can be world champion, and so if everyone else thought they were failures you'd have no one left on the grid."*
>
> Mark Webber

FUN FACTS ON BRAZILIAN GRAND PRIX

Brazil is the only country that bears no red hues in their flag among all the other Grand Prix hosts on the current Formula One calendar. The home advantage speaks true of the Brazilian drivers, as they have dominated in their home race; Emerson Fittipaldi, Nelson Piquet, Ayrton Senna and Felipe Massa won multiple times with Carlos Pace having a single victory registered next to his name. Brazilian drivers have also claimed the most pole positions (10) than any other nation's drivers since 1973. The 1991 Brazilian Grand Prix was Senna's homecoming at its best. The two-time world champion at the time had never tasted victory on his home soil and his car did not make it easy for him in that race. Senna suffered gearbox issues with 20 laps remaining and had to compromise his driving with his gear stuck in 6th through the twisty circuit. The Brazilian legend fought through the circumstances, and crossed the chequered flag under the rain to claim his first home victory with exhaustion. The adrenaline wore off and the home hero was left bone-tired and dehydrated; he lost as much as 3kg over the course of the race, and needed all the help he could to get out of his car.

WATCH

2008 Brazilian Grand Prix, 2010 Abu Dhabi Grand Prix, 2012 Brazilian Grand Prix, 2016 Abu Dhabi Grand Prix.

DID YOU KNOW

Fernando Alonso was captured by the camera looking gutted after losing the championship to Vettel in Brazil? Due to the camera work by the TV director and the live commentary, viewers were misled into thinking Alonso was looking towards Vettel, feeling the defeat. He was, however, looking at his former teammate, native Brazilian driver Felipe Massa, as it was his farewell race before retirement.

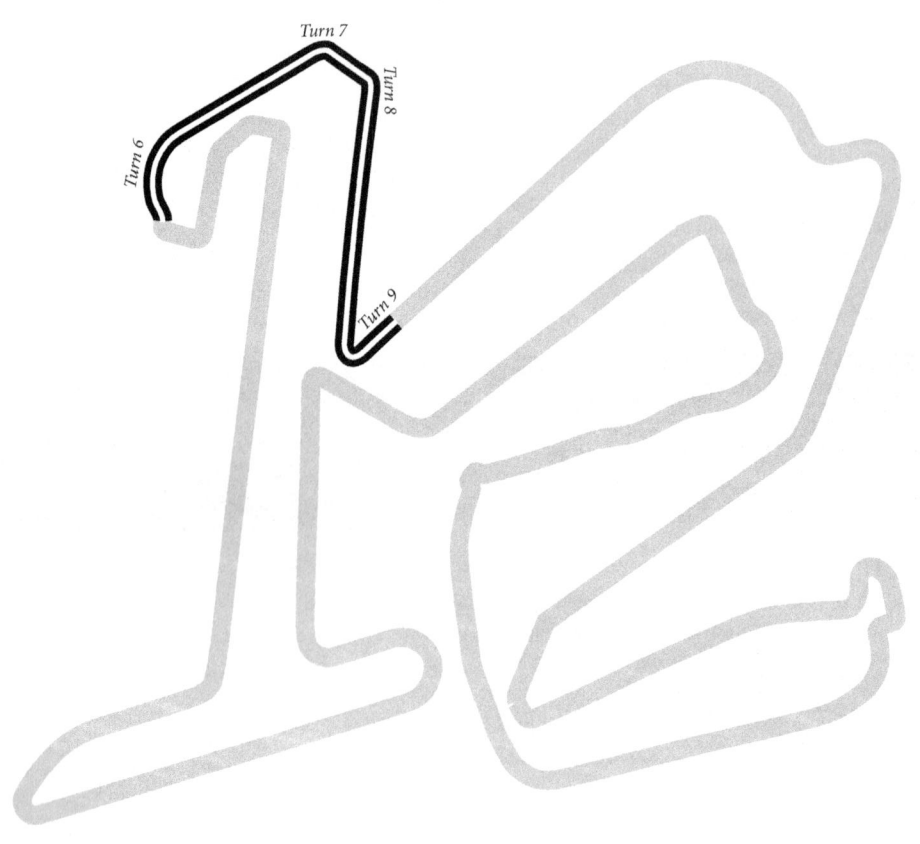

Turn 6
Turn 7
Turn 8
Turn 9

Sepang International Circuit

2.759639442277251, 101.73173458162044

RACE 8

2013 Malaysian Grand Prix

56 Laps

"This is silly, Seb...com'on."

When Number 2 is Number 1

Since 1999, Sepang International Circuit had been the host of the Malaysian Grand Prix, which is usually held between the end of March and early April each year. It is the first of many of Hermann Tilke's[1] fine works; 5.543km in length, consisting of 56 laps, two long straights, and a combination of 18 fast and slow corners. Malaysia's very humid weather usually reaches 40 degrees centigrade at the track and easily surpasses 50 degrees inside the cockpit; at other times you might be in luck for more chilling weather that produces some of the worst Monsoon downpours you can ever imagine.

Since 2006, I have been a regular attendee at the annual event and I have to say Sepang never fails to deliver for the fans. Therefore it was extremely sad to know the Malaysian Grand Prix Corporation and Formula One failed to reach an agreement to extend the contract beyond 2017. 18 years of glory came to an end when the curtain was drawn for the final time in October 2017.

---

1 Herman Tilke is one of four designers recognised by the FIA but has predominantly been the only one to be commissioned to design Formula One tracks.

I have many fond memories here, 13 races in 13 years, each proving to be as exciting as the others, if not more memorable. I have seen my favourite driver Kimi Räikkönen triumph in 2008 from P3. I have witnessed Lewis Hamilton's despair when his engine blew, smoked, set on fire and came to a halt in front of us, literally, parked at turn 1. Not to forget the first "half-point race" of the 21st century, when the race was red-flagged after lap 31 due to torrential rain; the downpour could not cool the fans, furious for a refund. I also remember Fernando Alonso winning in an underperforming machine in wet and wild conditions in 2012 from P14; it was nail biting down to the wire, and the race result may have been different had Sauber's Sergio Pérez not cracked under pressure. My very last visit in 2016, I got to see Daniel Ricciardo win and celebrate with his signature shoey[2] on the top step of the podium.

Flashback to one of those memorable Sunday afternoons at Sepang. I was eagerly waiting in my seat in the grandstand overlooking the main straight with turns 1 and 2, and to my left, some gaps of the uphill climb between turns 3 and 4. The ringside seat in the house, I called it. It took me a couple of years of roaming and researching to find this spot as the best among all other seating areas, bettering the more expensive main grandstand in front of the start straight/pit lane view. Here I got to see most of the action when cars came towards you at 315kph, coming out of the slipstream from the car in front and making that lunge from the inside of turn 1 to make the pass. The other car would get to fight back by manoeuvring for a better entry into the inside line of turn 2. It was as good as you can get for an RM333.00 grandstand ticket at an early bird price; merely a fraction of the price you pay for the main grandstand tickets.

On that March Sunday afternoon in 2013, the race got underway on a damp track, with Red Bull's triple world champion at the time, Sebastian Vettel, leading the pack into turn 1 from his 38th pole position. Five lights

2 Shoey refers to the podium celebration by drinking champagne from a shoe. This is a signature act performed by Daniel Ricciardo.

out and the cars got away fine, they swung pass turns 1 and 2 in front of us in orderly fashion. No drama yet. By the time the pack had made their way back to the start-finish line again, I saw Red Bull's Mark Webber and Ferrari's Alonso going wheel to wheel. Before I could gather my thoughts, I saw sparks coming out from Ferrari's front wing, then snap! Alonso's front wings broke and wedged underneath the car, his F138 skidded uncontrollably towards turn 1, towards the gravel trap, towards us. The broken wing was deemed terminal. There was no turning back for the Spaniard once he was that deep into the gravel trap; race over. We got up close to the champion, but perhaps not an ideal way for most Tifosis[3].

The race settled itself after a few more laps before the track began drying up quickly, opening up pit windows for dry rubber around lap 6. The second round of pit stops at around lap 28 saw the cars shuffling for positions, a bit of musical chairs on the asphalt. This was a tricky time sorting out cars back in the old days when you were without any electronic aid to assist you with the packing order. Drivers will be applying different strategies and it was difficult to know outright without the TV commentary. You could figure out who was on hard or soft rubber by the colour stripes on the tyres but that was pretty much it. There were on-site speakers that overhung the grandstand ceiling; the volume and the quality was nothing to shout about, and the commentary came in a mix of Bahasa Malay and English, catering to both the local and foreign fans. Most of the time it was commentary on the positions of the cars, and more of a noise than anything you would pay attention to, especially when you have 20 2.4 litres V8 engines taking their turns creating symphonies for all their money's worth.

On that fateful Sunday though, we saw Red Bull's Webber taking a decent lead over his teammate Vettel after their respective pit stops. After lap 40, it seemed like the Red Bulls had again held serve over their main rivals, and another one-two finish was very much in the bag. Their closest rivals,

3 Tifosi is Italian referring to the Ferrari supporters.

Hamilton and Nico Rosberg of Petronas Mercedes, were P3 and P4 respectively, unlikely to make any threat on the day with their performance. Given the circumstances, Webber should pace himself and bring the car home. *'Theoretically, the race is over for the front runners, let's pay some attention to the midfield battle'*, I remember saying to myself. Boy was I wrong in thinking that! His teammate Vettel seemed to close in on Webber lap by lap.

Now this is interesting, the two have never enjoyed each other's companies since day one. Webber called Vettel the 'kid' zoning in on his inexperience when the German's Toro Rosso STR2 crashed into the Aussie's RB3 in 2007 under the safety car period, wiping both cars out for potentially their team's first-ever podium in Fuji, Japan. It was the first of many crashes and clashes they have come together on and off the track, and let's just say they have never seen eye to eye since.

This is exactly what Formula One fans are after, rivalries and battles on tracks, drivers mastering their overtaking or defending moves. That is what thousands pay to come and see live, and there I was, about to witness another great internal bullfight. In my far-right sights, at the Hibiscus-looking grandstand, I could see both cars coming around the last corner, turn 15, a tight left-hand hairpin, then exit with full throttle across the start-finish line for the 46th time. Vettel was in Webber's gearbox and took the slipstream that was on offer, pulled out to his right, and tried to dive down the inside; Webber was particularly aggressive, stuck his elbows out and pushed Vettel almost towards the pit wall. It looked like the two almost touched, but they did not. If they had, it could have been catastrophic for all parties concerned.

Crowds around me were elevated to get a closer glimpse of the action, the oohs and aahs volumised from our grandstand, amplifying the nearby surround sound. I thought Webber's move was a bit harsh and untidy; the

Australian could have spared more rooms to be fair. Vettel persisted in a series of nifty moves, went nip and tuck and eventually made the move stick and stayed ahead of his teammate for the remaining 11 laps to cross the chequered flag to claim his 27th career victory. The Red Bulls were followed by the two Mercedes, Hamilton and Rosberg, a great showing for the Petronas branded "home" team, something worth cheering for from the local crowd.

The German had started on pole and won on merit. So I thought. The wheel to wheel combat was a good spectacle for the fans, but not so pleasing to the Red Bull's management, apparently. Yes, both cars came home safely, as Red Bull secured another one-two finish, with car number 1 (Vettel) finishing on the top step of the podium ahead of car number 2 (Webber) second.

The Revelation

At the end of every race, the top three drivers will park their cars at parc fermé[4] for scrutiny. Generally, the drivers will congratulate each other and mingle with the team members who are barricaded around the cars. Drivers will then enter the pit building for weighing before heading into the green room[5]. In that small room, a camera crew will be present to capture moments of the top three drivers catching a breath or hydrating before heading out for the podium ceremony. It is a very interesting 5-minute time span where we get to see the drivers' interaction with one another, post-race style.

In this instance, Vettel was obviously the happiest bloke in the room, wearing a big smile on his face chatting with Red Bull's chief designer Adrian Newey, the mastermind behind so many championship-winning cars from past to present. Moments later, Webber came into the room and

---

4 Parc fermé originated in French, literally meaning "closed park", is a secure area at a motor racing circuit wherein the cars are driven back to the pits post race.

5 Green room also known as the cool down room is usually situated nearby the rostrum, it is a small room designed to allow the podium finishers to rest and prepare for podium ceremony.

sat himself down while the camera zoomed in on him. Webber took a sip out of his drink bottle.

"Multi 21 Seb?" He questioned.

"Yeah, Multi 21." He concluded.

He pushed away his bottle in frustration. The camera turned to Vettel for his reaction as he was chucking down a bottle of water prepared by the event organiser; sucking down the cheap plastic bottle in full force to hydrate his body after losing as much as 3 litres of fluid from the race under the humid weather. As an afterthought, Vettel was trying to avoid the conversation, while Newey was sandwiched between the pair and had nothing to offer. An awkward silence instantly pervaded the room.

Multi 21? The TV audience was puzzled. It all came under the sun during the podium interview when Webber spilt the beans on how the team had ordered both drivers to dial down the machines to bring the cars home safely as per race order. However their number 1 driver (Vettel) decided to do otherwise, but his actions will always be protected, as usual. And so the story unfolded as the egocentric self had gotten the best of Vettel and he had disobeyed team orders for his own personal gain under broad daylight. For most Formula One fans out there, they will remember this as the race that went down in history as the infamous 'multi 21' or 'multi two-one'.

> *"In fact, managing donkeys is sometimes easier than managing drivers."*
>
> Christian Horner

Multi 21 Saga

Formula One teams, engineers and drivers converse during the race using tons of jargon, some very technical; others are more common to the TV audience at large. Every team will develop a completely random set of codes to communicate with their drivers to avoid other teams picking up any intel that could benefit rivals. Ferrari uses Italian on some occasions in their radio messages, just to bypass any eavesdropping from other teams. And trust me, every team has assigned staff to keep tabs on their rival teams' radio messages. Multi 21 is code for the Red Bull team to decipher as 'number two driver over number one", also known as "team orders". Team order is a form of warranty or insurance in the best interests of the team for maximizing results for races. In this very incident in Malaysia, Multi 21 was broadcast as a code to ask Vettel and Webber to hold their positions, manage both cars and bring home the maximum points for the weekend. It may seem contradictory to the nature of competition asking drivers not to race each other, but remember, Formula One is a team sport after all.

The radio messages that were released post-race are as follows:

(Vettel closed in on Webber)

RB Team Engineer: *"Careful Sebastian, careful."*

RB Team Engineer: *"Sebastian, multi map two one, multi map two one, and look after your tyres please."*

Horner: *"Come on Sebastian, you need to give him the space. Hold position."*

(Vettel Overtook Webber)

Horner: *"This is silly Seb, com'on."*

Webber: *"Yeah, that's good teamwork."*

RB Team: *"Okay Mark, he was told. He was told."*

RB Team: *"Sebastian…"*

Vettel: *"I was really scared. Main straight, all of sudden he was moving and I had to leave the line. To repeat, I had to get over the line. He didn't leave me any space."*

(Chequered flag)

Horner: *"Good job Sebastian. Good job. It looked like you want it bad enough. Still there will be explaining to do."*

Life Lesson #8

All About Perspective

Without the radio message and the revelation from the post-race interview, the race would appear to have been what I just thought I saw; even the SkySport commentators covering the race were only second-guessing what might have happened. Ted Kravitz, the pit lane reporter for the network did speculate that something unusual had happened when the only radio message picked up at the time was Red Bull's team boss Christian Horner saying *"This is silly Seb"*, but nothing concrete lead anyone to believe it was referring to the team order at the time. Only after Webber's green room frustration, they started to gather there was more to the race; Vettel had stolen Webber's thunder.

Having stationed myself at one spot for the entire race, with the vantage point kept to just several corners at best, it did not help to uncover the whole race as it was. There is always the other side of the story, whether it is an open door secret or closed-door affair, there are always two sides of the coin; it is called perspective. I was totally dumbfounded leaving the circuit to find the insight afterwards. Life is about understanding perspective, not necessarily always taking the right one, but giving yourself a chance to get an overview before jumping the gun. I was quick to jump to the conclusion that Webber did not seize his chance when he had the lead while trying to push Vettel to the wall. That was what I saw, but not what I knew.

In life, we are often blinded by the media, so much so we are easily led onto a bandwagon. Media is probably at its peak in terms of being influential in our decision-making; we are being exposed and fed in this fast-paced world with information on a day-to-day basis. So fast so we had little chance to investigate further on the genuineness of the information. What we decide to believe to be genuine, which sides we take, can often be the difference in making us happy or sad, obese or slim, peaceful or fearful, philosophical or suicidal.

In all honesty, what we should do more often is to question and to give the benefit of the doubt. This sounds like a contrary statement; to question yet to give others the benefit of the doubt sounds rather paradoxical. Context is important. Without context, the story has little meaning. It is like watching highlights of the overtaking but not understanding the significance behind the moves in terms of championship standings; the overtaking manoeuvre will present a different value.

"Perspective is a moment in time that cannot be fully appreciated until that moment has passed."

Tibor Kalman

The Donut Story

We need to question the information we are fed, seeking its genuineness; the truth behind closed doors, do our part by asking the right questions. They say you are what you eat, you are what you think. I would not say perspective is everything but it plays an indicative role. The perspective we take can determine the values we receive and, in turn, lead us to different outcomes. An interesting YouTube video that went viral in recent years had a particularly good plot that saw it being reproduced in various versions. The outline of the story remains the same, only the characters and the subject was substituted. The version I first watched was about the man and the donuts.

The video was narrated from the person's point of view, and it read as follows:

"So I am at the airport and they have got this deal for five donuts for $5, which is an awesome deal because it's pretty much the same price as buying three donuts. Anyway so it doesn't matter. I sat myself down and I picked up the paper and started reading the paper and this guy sits down across from me. I look over the paper and he kind of gives me a bit of a smile and I give him a bit of a nod and go back to reading the business section. A little while later I hear this rustling on the table and I am like...and I look over and the guy has got his hand in the bag of the donuts. Okay that's a bit weird, but it doesn't really matter, the guy looks like he is homeless, he probably needs them more than I do. I've still got four donuts anyway and I'm not gonna eat all four donuts so what do I care. So I reached in the bag and grabbed a donut and started eating it and then I went back to reading the paper. So I'm just getting into the social pages and I hear this rustling on the table again and I look over and the guys got his hand into the bag of donuts, again! He takes a bite and I am like 'what the crap?' Now I am getting a bit angry, but the precedent has been set so I don't feel like I can say anything. But I reach in the bag a bit more aggressively and I take a bite and I just shake my head like 'whatever'. So a few minutes have gone

by and there's this call over the loudspeaker for the next departure, and the guy gets up and starts gathering all of his stuff. As he gets to the end of the table he stops, and I see him out of the corner of my eye, and he reaches into the bag and he pulls out the last donut, and I am like 'seriously?' And he looks at me and he breaks it into two and he hands it to me. I reach out and take this half in total disbelief and he kind of nods at me and he walks off. So, while I am sitting here pondering on the absurdity of what's just happened, I hear my flight called, so I get up and grab my bag and I grab my jacket, and under my jacket is MY bag of donuts. Not only was I eating that guy's donuts the whole time, and he didn't say anything, he took out his last donut and broke it in half and gave it to me."

Whether this was a genuine incident or fiction, it has good moral for the purpose of sharing a good sense of perspective. Rightly so, situations as such happen frequently in our lives, with or without us noticing it. Some of us tend to jump to conclusions to judge quicker than others and sometimes find ourselves in an awkward situation afterwards. Should we ask more questions and assess ourselves in the situation, giving others the benefit of the doubt? There is a fine line between giving others the benefit of the doubt, because you simply do not want to overdo it to a point and allow others to abuse it; take advantage of you or use it against you.

> ## *"When you change the way you look at things, the things you look at change."*
> Wayne Dyer

In the grand scheme of things, the loser of the 2013 Malaysian Grand Prix is ironically the team that won the race on Sunday, Red Bull Racing. Despite winning on paper with a one-two finish and taking home maximum points and prize money, they lost control over the management of their drivers, failing to manage what seemed to be a frosty relationship between their drivers for a few seasons too long. They lost the respect and trust between their two lead drivers. The team dynamic had been a distraction to the team, to say the least. Whilst Vettel was the official winner recognised by the FIA, Red Bull knew that the victory had genuinely been Webber's, therefore, the team actually financially awarded both drivers with winning bonuses. You cannot make an omelette without breaking some eggs and in Red Bull's case, they had to pay more than what they needed to in order to move forward. Well, at least to keep their number 1 driver happy and I believe Vettel even got away with a slap on the wrist. That is some perspective for us to digest.

> ## *"In the end it doesn't matter who sits next to me, I would beat them all."*
> Max Verstappen

FUN FACTS ON TEAM ORDER

Interestingly, in the same race, Mercedes handed out a team order requesting Rosberg to stay behind Hamilton, when the German driver was faster and eager to pass his teammate. Team boss Ross Brawn on the radio denied him the chance. Rosberg played by the team, and reminded them he was doing it for the team in contrasting style to what had happened with the Red Bull camp, who were running ahead of the Mercedes boys. Team order in Formula One does not usually happen early in the year; in Malaysia's case, it was only the second race of the season. Traditionally teams usually instruct team order during later stages when they have determined which of the two drivers has more chance of fighting for the championship. The infamous team order long-lived in Formula One fans' memory is none other than the one between Ferrari, Schumacher and his wingman Barrichello in 2002. Barrichello was asked to let Schumacher by and did so on the last corner of the last lap in the Austrian Grand Prix. Schumacher was not proud of the win and offered the top step of the podium on the rostrum, an act that was later fined by FIA. Schumacher did return the favour by his own decision to slow down his Ferrari and let Barrichello win the US Grand Prix that same year. The two crossed the line within a record margin of 0.011 seconds, the closest winning margin with a deliberate effort.

WATCH

2013 Malaysian Grand Prix, 2002 Austrian Grand Prix, 2010 German Grand Prix.

DID YOU KNOW

Mark Webber holds the record for the most races (130) before a maiden victory? The Queanbeyan native came close a few times in the 2009 season, before claiming his long-awaited win at Nürburgring in the German Grand Prix in a well-deserving manner.

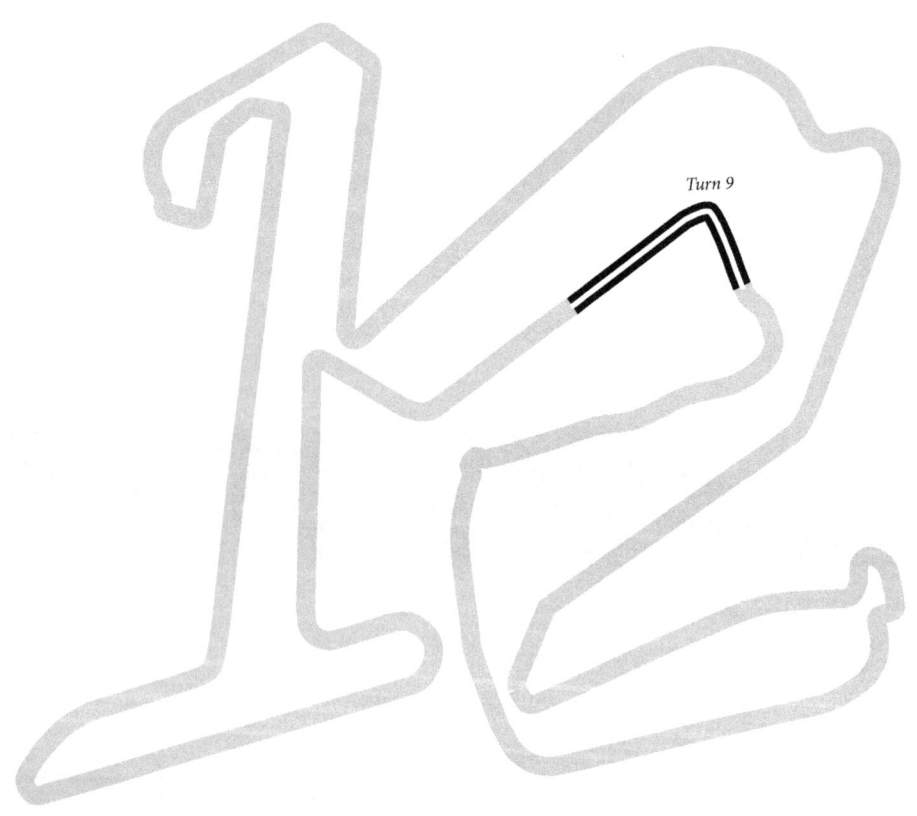

Turn 9

Marina Bay Street Circuit

1.2917429562472773, 103.86389896812541

RACE 9

2013 Singapore Grand Prix

61 Laps

"Obviously I didn't give them the most exciting race but on days like this, I really don't mind."

The Night Out

Since cutting ties with Malaysia and declaring their independence in 1965, Singapore has proved to be the economic powerhouse of Asia. A country small enough to self-sustain and pave ways in infrastructure development and innovations. Yes, they were once part of Malaysia, and now they are known as The Republic of Singapore. They have since proved their divorce with Malaysia, now their neighbour; indeed, a wise move.

While their neighbour gave birth to their first Formula One race in 1999, it was only a matter of time before the Singaporeans followed suit. This modern country, known as the lion city, finally made its roar and caught up with the Formula One train in 2008, staging the inaugural Singapore Grand Prix at the Marina Bay Street Circuit. The Singapore Grand Prix is dubbed as the "Monaco of Asia"; the street circuit comparable to the historic Monte Carlo race. The USP, unique selling point for Singapore's take, however, was not trying to replicate the impression of that of Monaco. To simply emulate the vibes of the street circuit from the principality would be disrespectful to the competitive nature of Singaporeans. They are, after all, the leaders of innovation and infrastructure in the contemporary setting.

Night racing was the deal for Singapore. To distinguish their race from the rest, they planned, designed then installed 1,600 lighting projectors to illuminate the track. Night racing only became a thing after Singapore proved to us again, that they are a wise bunch. Upon the success of the first-ever night race, fighting off all the technical obstacles and challenges to bring the race under lights, it has remained a night race, as much as for tradition as broadcaster cache. The timing of the night race in Asia allowed the British and European viewers to catch a traditional Sunday afternoon slot. Let's not forget, the United Kingdom was the founding place for Formula One racing and still holds a huge fan base in this region. With that in mind, Singapore's night race killed two birds with the one stone.

If you did not skip any chapters from this book, then you would know that I have covered three races from the 2012 season. The reason is simple. 2012 was arguably one of the most exciting years in Formula One's 70-year history, and I could have easily gone with more races without a cap. If 2012 was the finest ever, its successor, 2013 did not fare well at all in terms of competition. Three-time world champion Sebastian Vettel cruised and won races effortlessly from my point of view. He and his new love affair, RB9, Hungry Heidi, indeed kept their hunger to win, and absolutely blitzed the grid. He did not finished a race below P4, apart from one DNF at the British Grand Prix. And, wait for it, his wins tallied to a staggering 13 from 19 Grand Prix entries. Okay, let's be fair, he technically stole one from his teammate Mark Webber in Malaysia, so perhaps it should be 12 wins, not 13. Regardless, that was as impressive as it looked. His late-season form converted into nine consecutive wins, bagging lots of dollars in his bank. In any given year, with that many wins, that was enough to win two world championships.

The season might not have been as boring as hell if you were either German or Austrian, but the truth of the matter is, it was difficult to watch race after race seeing the same bloke on the top of the podium, and hearing the same two national anthems (one for the team, one for the driver). The season was as dull as dishwater. It was a stranglehold at the top, reminiscent of season 2002[1] with Schumacher and Ferrari. In a nutshell, on many occasions, I had the urge to turn off my TV before the race ended, but Formula One, after all, was and still is an indulgence for me that capped off Sunday before facing Monday blues.

So, what is so special about the 2013 Singapore Grand Prix? It was a special outing for team Vettel.

Sunday 22nd September 2013, 8 pm local time, while most people were getting ready for work or Monday school, more than 80,000 souls flocked trackside at Marina Bay. The street was about to come alive, with 22 of the world's best cars and drivers ready for battle, not under the scorching sun but artificial illumination. The humidity and track temperature remained intensely high from the start no less for the drivers as the crowd. The stunning overhead shot from the helicopter camera glanced through the high-rise skyline against a well-lit racing circuit, outlining the 23 corners with glow. It did more than justify Singapore's race as one of a kind.

The grid for the night saw Vettel on pole, with compatriot Nico Rosberg of Mercedes alongside him on P2. A surprising Frenchman, Romain Grosjean of Lotus, started behind Vettel on P3 and Red Bull's Mark Webber on P4. Followed by Lewis Hamilton of Mercedes, Felipe Massa and Fernando Alonso of Ferrari and Jenson Button of McLaren to round off the top eight. Vettel had claimed pole position the previous night, only one-tenth quicker over Rosberg. It was not a case where the two cars were closely

1 2002 was a season dominated by Michael Schumacher and Ferrari. Ferrari won 15 out of the 17 races, with Schumacher top honours 11 times, setting the most win record at the time while scoring 89.4% of all possible points in 2002. Schumacher finished every race on a podium, a 100% strike rate that will be hard to match anytime soon, and won his fifth titles with six races to spare. He enjoyed a 67-point margin over the second-place teammate in Ruben Barrichello.

matched, rather, Vettel opted for a single run during his Q3 qualifying
while the rest set their personal fastest times through multiple runs.

Lights out and it was a mad dash towards turn 1; Singapore fans were
treated with spark showers from the cars bottoming and streaking on the
surface of Marina promenade. Rosberg had a strong start and fancied his
chances, negotiating the battle by putting his nose alongside Vettel then
forcing his way ahead of his compatriot. For probably less than a split
second. His F1 W04 overcommitted and could not slow down quickly
enough through the corner and ran wide, allowing Vettel back into the
lead. That was a cringe moment for all anti-Vettel fans out there. The
German, the one in the blue Red Bull, took off like there was no tomorrow,
and never looked back. The other German, Rosberg saw the gap, went
for it, but overcooked it. Even if he had not, he was still subject to Vettel's
supremacy for 70 gruelling laps. I was not prepared to take any bets on that!

It was proven just less than two hours later; Vettel and Hungry Heidi were
an unbeatable couple, hitting all the apexes and having a bit of solitude
for much of the race. They danced through the backdrop of the scenic
Marina Bay and had not put a foot wrong all night. As they crossed the
chequered flag, fireworks saluted the German by illuminating the sky of
the lion city to celebrate his 33rd career victory in his 114th race entry. His
performance was stratospheric from lights to flag. Despite the victory, fans
were unimpressed by seeing yet another dominant performance from the
German champion; the post-race interview on the rostrum in Singapore
and the previous round in Monza turned out to be booing sessions.

*"Obviously I didn't give them the most exciting race but on days like this,
I really don't mind."* Vettel responded in a post-race interview. The German
was depressingly fast for the fans' liking, and they made their displeasure
heard loud and clear in front of the global audience.

"It was like we were running on the propeller and they were running on a jet plane. They just have so much downforce." Lewis Hamilton commented during the 2013 season proving just how superior Red Bull's cars were compared to the rest of the grid.

Cannot blame the fans for expressing their displeasure; after all, they had paid big bucks to see the thrills and spills, wheel to wheel action, captivating races that Formula One claims to offer. What they got in return, for most of the season, was simply a one-man show. Vettel became a villain when he piled on his wins and upgraded room for his trophy collections. In Singapore, Vettel won the race by an enormous margin, 32 seconds from Alonso at P2; the biggest winning margin for the track record. Rosberg started P2 and finished P4 with 50 seconds adrift. It was not simply a race win, it was a remarkable Grand Slam or 'Grand Chelem' in French. In Formula One terminology, this refers to the driver achieving the ultimate glory in a Grand Prix weekend; securing pole position, fastest lap, leading every lap and, last but not least, claiming race victory. Vettel's masterstroke was not solely down to the maturity of his race craft, at least that is not what I believe. Last season in 2012, Hungry Heidi's predecessor Abbey had been indestructible in Brazil, finishing the race with open wounds. If that was anything to go by, then Hungry Heidi was even more drilled, more refined, inches more towards perfection in design and most notably...more balanced.

Life Lesson #9
Balancing Act

Balance is a word we often hear in conversation, from drivers to engineers and mechanics. Not the physical balance where the car is heavier from one side to another, balance is an objective every Formula One team tries to accomplish through their machines. Balance is where the car performs on the track going at the limit of physics in both extreme measures in speed; both corners and straight lines. Which gets me to my next point. Top speed in a straight line versus fast cornering speed is two sides of the coin, a dilemma faced by drivers and engineers every Grand Prix weekend. The car can be set up for top straight-line speed but it will compromise on corners, slowing the car down relatively. Choosing to set up the cars for speeding through the corners will subsequently slow the car down in a straight-line attack. They simply cannot have it both ways. What they look for is finding the threshold that will provide the ultimate lap time that is suitable to the track and their strategic plan; the threshold that provides balance.

Downforce and Drags

Here comes the rocket science part of the sport, and I intend to explain this in as little words as I can. The science of Formula One cars is everything about the theory of aerodynamics. Aerodynamics is what makes planes take off and fly, working against and with air pressure to project the plane or the subject matter in the air. Formula One cars utilise aerodynamic theory opposite to the plane. Instead of pushing the plane into the sky, the Formula One car's objective is to use the same air pressure to push the car onto the floor, this is known as "downforce" or negative lift. To create downforce, the angles of the front and rear wings determine how much air pressure is applied via speed to gain grip in return. Downforce allows the car to create grip on the asphalt, and limit the time the car bounces off in the air, losing lap time. The more downforce, the greater the grip, and the faster the car travels. You might have heard that Formula One cars are capable of driving upside down in a tunnel with the amount of downforce they generate through velocity. In theory, by the law of physics, the car will indeed be able to sustain its weight onto the roof while travelling at a speed of 200kph. Having said that, I have not known anyone trying to put this to the test, well, at least not that I know.

Anyway, a good downforce is essential for the car to steer into corners quicker and smoother. Simultaneously, in creating downforce, the car is also subject to "drag" in a straight line drive. Drag is the air resistance when the car is travelling forward. When the car is punching through the air, the airflow drags and slows the car down. An example of drag in another sport would be indoor track cycling. In this sport, in the team pursuit category, we see how the cyclist takes turns to ride at the front, while the team hides behind the lead rider to benefit from the tow. The three cyclists will rotate between themselves and take turns to take on the drag in order to manage their speed and the energy output from each member of the team.

Tow or slipstream in Formula One, a term you might be familiar with by now, is a low-pressure air passage created by the car in front. Slipstream can provide substantial advantage on the track, just google the 2019 Italian Grand Prix. Monza, the home of Tifosi and the host of the Italian Grand Prix, is known as the "Temple of Speed"; it has only 11 corners with multiple long straights, resulting in 84% throttle each lap, in other words, it is a low downforce track. With cars spending most of the time flooring their throttles and less time on the brakes, the slipstream effect becomes crucial and apparent, as the tow can provide about 0.5 to 0.7 seconds boost. During the qualifying session 3, the final nine cars head out for the shoot-out with just enough time on the clock to set for the final run. All cars were out on their out-lap slowly making their way to the start-finish line. All were hesitant to get the ball rolling as no one wanted to be the first car to lead the pack, providing the advantage for the car behind. Everyone deliberately slowed down to a point; Nico Hülkenberg of Racing Point even drove out to the escape route to avoid being the first car. Eventually, some drivers had enough and tried to overtake to get it going before they ran out of time. It was so ridiculous, how everything unfolded, with eight of the nine cars failing to make the cut to bank in their lap only because of trying to avoid drag or hoping to benefit from the tow.

Just how much of the wings or other parts of the chassis could affect drag and downforce? Webber once shared his experience during the Australian Grand Prix in 2007. The fuel flap on his RB3 failed to close and was left open during the race. The malfunction of a small part of the car was costing him 7% reduction in downforce, losing a chunk of lap time on track. In Formula One, to reach top speed through a straight line, downforce must be reduced to the minimum, meaning less angle with the wings that will fight against the wind resistance.

Now, you might be thinking, since we are talking about aerodynamics, what about the wind? Well, the wind plays a big part, and can be a significant determinant of direction. Wind can be either termed as headwind or tailwind. A headwind will create more resistance when the car is travelling in straight-line speed while a tailwind will have the reverse effect and provide a boost to the speed of the car. Since the wind blows in one direction, this means that the car can be impacted by headwinds at one part of the circuit and tailwind at another section of the track. Engineers and drivers need to work out the car setup to capitalise on the wind effect.

To make a long story short on aero setups, having lesser downforce will gain in top speed but lessen grip through the twisty part of the circuit. On the other hand, having higher downforce sacrifices top speed but provides a better drive through the corners. Downforce and drag are just the basic gist of how Formula One cars operate. Factors other than the wing setup contribute to the overall performance of the car; these variables may include tyre compound, tyre pressure, weight distribution, fuel loads, ride height, brake balance, camber, gear ratios, differential, suspension, and the list goes on. It is not as simple as finding the perfect combination, the set up needs to be tuned to the driving styles of each individual driver versus the track characteristics. Therefore a set up that might work for driver A might not work as well for driver B. This makes it even far more challenging to work out the right formula and achieve a grand slam feat.

"I think Formula One is - there's a lot of differences from track to track, grip levels, tyre compound, so you always have to press the reset button and work from scratch again."

Lance Stroll

In life, it is all about finding the right balance to achieve perfect harmony. Everyone will have their own recipe that works in terms of lifestyle, health, career, relationships, spiritual journey and many more. To live to an optimal level and be efficient about our performance versus time, we need balance. We cannot be working 20 hours a day and expect to have quality time with our family or vice versa. Put simply, you cannot have your cake and eat it too. In this fast-paced world, work-life balance is getting a great deal of attention; employers understand that, in order to get the best out of their employees, they need a healthy and balanced lifestyle. Therefore, many companies these days offer various benefits in terms of health regimes, from free gym to regular social events to get them into the best possible shape, mentally and physically. While work-life balance has become a standard feature in many job ads, how much do we know to achieve this balance in our own right?

"It's not what you add that enriches your life - it's what you omit."

Rolf Dobelli

Negative Space

I am a designer by training and I have been practising as a graphic designer since 2003. In graphic design, there is a term we often use called "negative space" or, in more layman's terms "white space". White space, like the name suggests, is the area you see in a design piece that is purposely left blank. A space that is designed to be there to provide breathing space so that the rest of the design elements can work nicely together to convey the message. This is a design treatment to find the balance so we won't have every element shouting at us at the same time. Whilst the client might want to fill the page with information, trying too hard to do too many things on the canvas usually backfires and fails to deliver the message properly. In design, it is never about adding more but subtracting to find the right balance. By the same token, we need white space in our life to balance the chaos that we might be subject to from not only just our work, but family, relationships and everything in between. Having white space for ourselves grants us breathing space and an opportunity to express our life better on canvas.

> ## *"Design is perfect when there is nothing more to take away."*
> ### Jussi Kapanen

The Mee Goreng Analogy

I always love to share my analogy of balance through the art of cookery. IndoMie, an Indonesia brand that was known to a worldwide audience with their product Mee Goreng, is by far the most down to earth instant noodles product that I know of. It is a product that I consume on a fortnightly basis and I learned to master the product while I was still a teen. This is my SOP for plating a perfect Mee Goreng for a late-night supper: first, unpack two packets of Mee Goreng, put the noodles into boiling water for about 4 minutes until they soften; drain the noodles but not totally, keeping some moist so they won't dry out too quickly; add the dry noodles, seasoning and fried shallots; give them a good toss, then add sweet soya sauce, chilli sauce and sautéed oil; put in everything except one packet of the chilli sauce, and blend. Plate and serve with a fried egg on the side.

That would be a perfectly balanced Mee Goreng, for me. I did not use the full amount of the chilli sauce because the spicy kick will tip the balance of flavour. I believe this was not the way Mee Goreng was intended to be seasoned, because after all, they did provide more chilli, but I only used half of the portion. For me, that was the right balance, and it might be different for another person. Likewise, when you google for recipes online, you can never follow them word for word, sometimes a tweak here and there will give you the right balance to meet your taste. In the kitchen, I only put in the right amount of the ingredient that will suit my palate, and that sometimes means having leftover uncooked ingredients on the chopping board. My argument is always the same; having too much overpowers and ruins the dish. It has to be balanced. By the same token, I do not endorse a diet that is one-dimensional. I believe our body needs a balanced diet with proteins, carbs and greens. The key is moderation in terms of food intake.

In my opinion, the key to a balanced life is how we decide to distribute our time. How we manage and prioritise time to rest, work and play. Trust me, it is not as simple as dividing them into equal shares. We may want to investigate how much we are investing in each of the categories and how much more we are getting in return. Work on the threshold. We might have more on our scale than just rest, work and play but, the important thing is, we weigh those in ourselves and adjust according to our needs and our desired lifestyle. It is true work is important, getting the dollars rolling in, but sometimes, we need to know where the boundaries are and not let work dictate our life or any other things to creep into our white space.

"Balance makes perfect harmony."
Wu Bai

Nobody can come up with a perfect plan to tune us for a balanced lifestyle but ourselves. We all have preferences in terms of what we value, and these are just like the driving styles of Formula One drivers; their ways to approach the corners and throttles off the track vary from one driver to another. Our lives are different in terms of our needs and wants, and we need to make adjustments or adaptations to make ends meet. Indeed, like tweaking and tuning the car to our specification to make it work on a different circuit, we are just like the drivers, engineering our lives to cater for our needs in a balanced manner. Balance is a form of practice and when we know we have achieved the optimum, the balance in life, we will ultimately feel fulfilled.

Hungry Heidi had fulfilled her destiny, she was a well-oiled machine. Adrian Newey, the chief designer, had risen to the technical challenge year after year for the Austrian squad and developed yet another winning machine with perfection in balance. So balanced was Hungry Heidi that she was excellent in adapting to many circuits with various characteristics. She was indeed in a league of her own, breaking the most consecutive wins (9) record, previously held by the two Ferrari legends in Michael Schumacher and Alberto Ascari. On top of that, she had the highest title margin at 155 points. But remember, Hungry Heidi was perfect for Vettel, the pair complemented each other and bonded for a perfect partnership. Vettel was able to work with her and make the car talk. This was the right balance for Vettel and we are searching for that right balance for ourselves.

Nobody is here to tell us how to live our lives, find the right balance or cook Mee Goreng the right way. We are on our own to find that balance; the journey to get the best of both worlds.

"Some Italians are geniuses, but you have to find a balance."
Alain Prost

FUN FACTS ON SINGAPORE GRAND PRIX

Marina Bay Street Circuit, like every other street circuit on the Formula One calendar, is subject to high probability of safety car intervention. The Singaporean Grand Prix has featured safety car deployment in every single race since inducted to the calendar in 2008. In provision, strategists are always busy calculating and forecasting the best plan before and during the race. With this in mind, former Renault team boss Flavio Briatore orchestrated a master plan to order their second driver Nelson Piquet Jr to crash deliberately during the race to help teammate Fernando Alonso to gain track position with the safety car intervention in play. Alonso, as planned, inherited the race lead after an atypical pit stop prior to the crash. He held on to the lead and seemingly won the race, at the time known to be a pure stroke of luck. The crash-gate allegation only surfaced a year after Renault sacked Piquet from the team. The race-fixing scandal was costly for Briatore, who was banned from Formula One and any other FIA event indefinitely.

WATCH

2013 Singaporean Grand Prix, 2014 Malaysian Grand Prix.

DID YOU KNOW

Sebastian Vettel made his Formula One debut with BMW Sauber in the 2007 United States Grand Prix at Indianapolis? He got the nod to stand in for lead driver Robert Kubica after the Polish driver suffered from concussion sustained from a shunt in Canada.

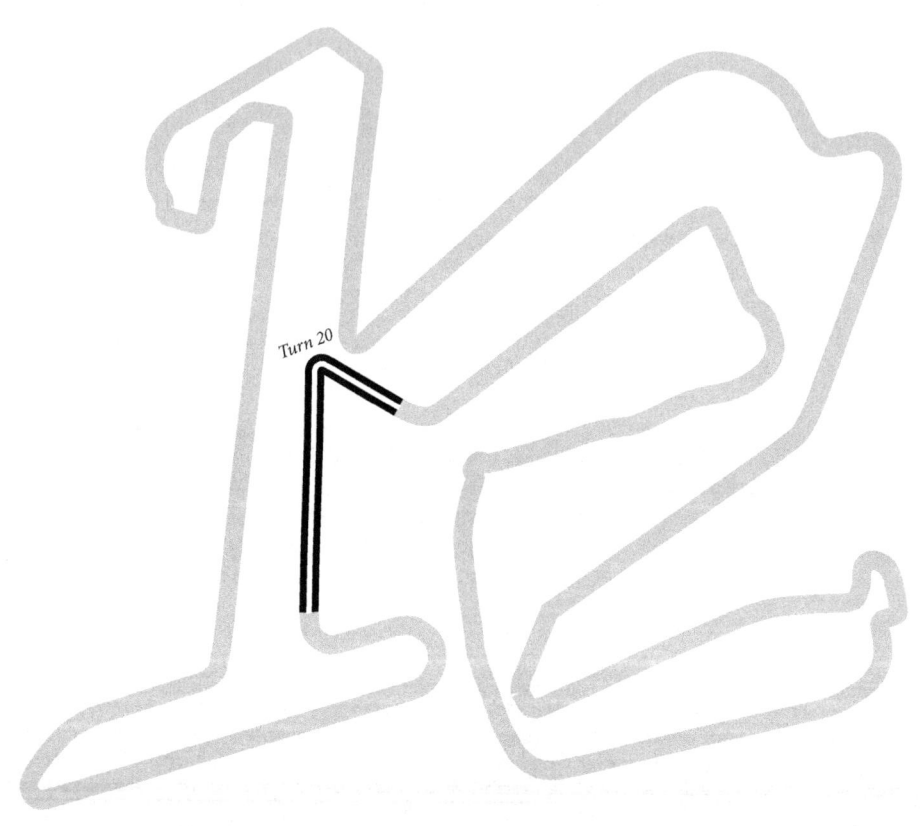

Turn 20

Circuit of the Americas

30.134812752037476, -97.63587256030492

RACE 10

2015 United States Grand Prix

56 Laps

"I don't know what the hell that was."

Friends then Foes

Out of the 20 races on a typical Formula One calendar, Canada, United States, Mexico and Brazil are the stops that I was not willing to watch live. You would probably figure by now that these are the races that take place on the other side of the Pacific Ocean. Traditionally, Formula One races always commence on a Sunday afternoon regardless of which continent they take place, bar Singapore and Abu Dhabi being the two that host races as night and twilight features. That just means, for a few weekends each year, these American continent races will be broadcast at a very awkward time for me and those who live in Asia or the Asia Pacific. I did, however, stay up for a couple of Brazilian Grand Prix, namely 2007, 2008 and 2012, which were all title deciders cum season finales. Those three races surely deserved or worthy of a late nighter; all nail biters in their own right, if I have not mentioned it already.

Circuit of the Americas, the host of the United States Grand Prix, has never stood tall against some of the traditional tracks like Interlagos or even its neighbouring partner Circuit Gilles Villeneuve in Canada. Season

2015 was by no means a fancy year worthy of any late-night races. It was a year where Lewis Hamilton dominated with his F1 W06 Hybrid[1]. The turbo-powered machine was fast from day one, claiming a massive haul of 17 podiums out of 19 scheduled races; an incredible feat that you do not get to see often. It was a boring stretch in terms of competitions for Formula One, unless you were British or a fan of the Mercedes AMG Petronas Formula One Team. It was just a year that failed to live up to its hype or expectations. The possible highlight in terms of driver's drama probably would come down to the United States Grand Prix.

It was the 16th out of a 19-race calendar, with three races to spare Hamilton could be crowned world champion for the fourth time in his illustrative career. He had that kind of lead, and it was that kind of year; a one-horse race too easy to predict. The weather in Austin was not as predictable as the season, with tropical storm Patricia trying to be a party crasher in the background. The changing conditions over the race weekend meant qualifying was rescheduled to Sunday morning instead of the usual Saturday afternoon. Even by postponing the qualifying session 12 hours later, the rain from Patricia persisted and halted the standard three-session to just two.

The scenario was that Hamilton's teammate Nico Rosberg must win come rain or shine, to keep his championship hopes alive, mathematically speaking. But we knew far and wide that the championship was Hamilton's; it was just a matter of when and in which race. Nevertheless, Rosberg hit the nail on the head on a wet and wild Sunday morning, he took pole position, followed by Hamilton on the first row of the grid. Rosberg snatched pole by a slim margin of 0.105 second over his teammate and that was a decent effort for his championship aspirations. Spoiler alert: this pole position, however, was to be short-lived. Just hours after the qualifying session, the race kicked off on time. When the five lights went off, Hamilton

1 In 2014, FIA welcomed the Hybrid era when they introduced 1.6 litre turbocharged V6 power units to replace the aspirated 2.4 litre V8 engines.

erased all the hard work Rosberg had done in the morning and took the lead after the first corner.

> *"You can't win a race in the first corner, but you can lose it in the first corner."*
> Unkown

It was too early to sentence the German; after all, his car had only clocked a few hundred metres, while the race was still young, and hopefully not a long race for him. Rosberg managed to take back his lead around lap 18 and, with a few safety car interventions shaking up the order, he was back in the lead with just a handful of laps remaining with Hamilton breathing down his neck. His championship hopes were still alive as long as he could keep Hamilton honest. Come lap 48, out of nowhere, a sweaty moment for Rosberg when he lost it at turn 12; running deep, giving away the lead to his teammate, giving away another title to his fellow colleague. His championship hope, to follow his Finnish father's[2] footsteps, vanished into thin air.

"I don't know what the hell that was!" Frustrated at himself with an unforced error that was too costly to bear, it was later revealed that a strong gust of wind, the force of nature had pushed his car wide. By the sound of the wind, maybe it was fate or maybe the God of Formula One had spoken, Hamilton took full advantage of his teammate's cold feet moment, seized the lead and never looked back. He pushed his car hard and created some gaps between the German before crossing the chequered flag as a triple world champion. Rosberg brought home his exhausted W06, runner-up for the race and the season, missing out on yet another grand prize for the third consecutive year, and had to concede a gut-wrenching defeat due to his own liability.

2 Keke Rosberg is a Finnish World Champion winning his driver's title with Williams in 1982.

In the typical green room setup, towels and bottled drinks will be prepared on the table, alongside the Pirelli branded caps for the winner and runner-ups. For branding purpose, it has been a tradition for the podium finishers to wear these "tyre branded" caps for the podium ceremony before the crowd and for a wider global audience. In the past, when the competition was made up of multiple tyre suppliers, namely Bridgestones and Michelins, drivers would pick up their respective cap. Since 2007, when Formula One switched to a single tyre supplier Bridgestones then, with the inception of Pirelli in 2011, the caps all had the same branding, design and colours except the stitching on the sides that differentiated "1st", "2nd" and "3rd", to allow the drivers to pick up the correct cap.

The Cap-gate

Rosberg was probably more frustrated at himself than anyone, sinking his body on the white Le Corbusier armchair at one end the room; head hung and supported by his right arm, his body language said it all. His white racing suit almost worked as a camouflage to the chair to tell us how he wanted to hide from reality. He wanted no part of this, no part of the celebration. Watching his teammate crowned as world champion for the third successive year while celebrating together as a team was a cruel experience.

Hamilton, having spent time celebrating on the slow down lap and parc fermé came in minutes later; Rosberg stood up as Hamilton approached, the pair embraced to acknowledge another year-long battle had come to an end. After official weighing[3], a post-race protocol for all drivers, Hamilton took a few moments to allow what he had just accomplished sink in, kneeling on the floor, catching a breath. Momentarily he walked to the other side of the room to soak up his emotion. He then turned and found his Mercedes technical director Paddy Lowe before moving onto the long white table to pick up his winner's cap. Upon getting his Pirelli cap, he snatched the runner-up cap and threw it across the room; it landed perfectly on Rosberg's lap.

---

3 FIA requires all the drivers and cars to be weighed separately post-race to meet the minimum weight requirement and ensure no cars are racing underweight to gain an advantage.

All was nicely captured. It was a moment or a statement rather, that said, *"Here you go, number two."*

Rosberg, without much hesitation, tossed it back to his teammate.

Years later in an interview, Rosberg revealed that his loss in the United States in 2015 was a dark moment for him, as Hamilton was able to walk all over him, on and off the track, even in the cool down room. He took it on the chin and vowed to up his game. The German came back with a vengeance and won seven on the trot after that Texas debacle. In hindsight, the defeat was a career turning point for Rosberg.

Some may argue that the German was a sore loser and showed little sportsmanship. I have to disagree. Look, the man just lost a title fight he had worked so hard for. Give him a break and give him the space he deserved. He could have taken the cap himself, he did not need to be reminded. He certainly did not need to be reminded about his position in the race classification, in Mercedes's camp, or his final standing in the championship. The act was adding insult to injury, in my opinion.

> *"To be teammates in Formula One actually means you are first rivals, not really mates."*
>
> Asif Kapadia

Life Lesson #10
No Friendly Business

It was not hard to tell they had been foes ever since partnering up in the same team; no mind-reading required. The tension was high early on, with Hamilton declaring they were no longer friends after their first season together. The intra-team rivalry always gets a bit extra fiery when you are in the winning team with a competitive package. All eyes were on the duo, the pressure cooker was always on to kick each other's backside in every practice session, qualifying, race, even at times in various press conferences and PR stunts. Of course, it was never an overnight affair, the two got into each other's way and had on-track clashes where neither wanted to admit fault or claim responsibility. Many in fact; one too many in the team's point of view. It was a potent mix that sabotaged the team's result and caused it to lose a lot of dollars in between. Google Belgian 2014, Spain 2016, Austrian 2016 and they will keep you entertained.

It was not an overnight affair, I say this again because the two actually shared a lot while growing up karting together. Yes, they were good friends. They were good friends until Hamilton decided to leave McLaren and join forces. In hindsight, it was absolutely the right decision for Hamilton after winning multiple titles with the German constructor, on the other hand, the move cost him a friend with whom he had grown up.

Flashback to the 2008 season opener in Melbourne, Australia. Hamilton won the Australian Grand Prix in his McLaren MP-23, and coming P2 was none other than his karting mate Rosberg in his Williams FW30; identical to their finishing positions in the 2015 United States Grand Prix. What happened in the green room was nowhere near identical. The two young stars were captured in pure joy as the pair jumped into each other's arms with huge hugs and congratulations; the body language was full of genuine excitement for each other.

The two were living in a parallel universe until they began the experiment of sharing the same technology, innovations and support. How things quickly changed for them and how fragile their friendship was when conflict of interest was in place, with the tension between the pair boiling over more often than not. Their mutual relationship soon turned them to two embittered teammates. Winning leads to fame and fortune, and neither wanted to play second fiddle, especially when we are talking about two elite Formula One drivers, with highly competitive natures at the peak of their careers. Their dynamic was too strong a force that it quickly became detrimental for the team. Their so-called professional relationship was just ungovernable by the team management and irreparable among the duo.

It is not uncommon to have strained relationships with teammates in professional sports; rivals within a team are not patented solely by Formula One drivers. We have seen many instances when teammates turn against each other for all kinds of different reasons. In 2009, Gilbert Arenas and Javaris Crittenden of the Washington Wizards made the headline in the NBA, when they trash-talked each other by flashing their pistols in a showdown in the locker room; no shots were fired but the incident backfired and ruined both of their careers. In 2005, English Premier League players, Kieron Dyer and Lee Bowyer of Newcastle United had an on-field scuffle when Bowyer was crossed at his teammate for not passing him the ball. Punches were thrown while red cards handed out from the referee, throwing them out of the game. This one has a slightly better ending to it, as both continue their career and play together in the same team after leaving Newcastle United. Just google them and these tales will keep you entertained.

In life, I have learned to never mix business with pleasure. Never be involved in business propositions with friends or family. Never get too close to people you work with or work for. I have learned to keep a professional relationship with all my current, former colleagues and employers. I won't say everything is strictly business in every conversation, but I have set my boundaries and marked my lines fairly clearly. I understand that, in a typical 9 to 5 job, when one third of our day is spent at work, relationships are bound to form. Having said that, I believe there is nothing wrong just being a friendly colleague for eight hours per day with occasionally some water cooler chat, but nothing more. The moment you begin to share more than what is necessary, the dynamic changes and you will begin to jeopardize the situation. When the line is crossed and you are no longer just a colleague, expectation shifts and you might find yourself associating with them for the wrong reasons. Politics, red tape, hierarchy, conflicts of interest are the common traps people can easily suck into when workmates begin to take the prefix off and call you mate.

Let's not detail each of the traps, but the common one is clearly money. Money is the driving force in many circumstances, most noticed in the workplace. When we are at work, we are there for the money. Let's be honest, unless we are a full-time volunteer or philanthropist, we are there for the remuneration. So money is the culprit. Let's elaborate.

Most workplaces practice salary secrecy, it is an unwritten rule most are willing to obey with irony. Curiosity killed the cat, or let the truth be told, we all want to know how much our office neighbours take home every fortnight, but we are not willing to share the same info to them. Why? Because the mysterious figures printed on their payroll can either motivate or demoralise us. It is human nature to compete, we are born to compete. This is a risk most companies are not willing to take. The so-called unwritten rule is in place to create a more harmonic working environment, and stop workers fighting each other for better compensation for their time.

For Rosberg and Hamilton, it might not have been money, directly. They were fighting for the ultimate success, and success on the track at the end of the day did lead to prize money.

> *"Not everyone at your workplace is your friend. Do your job. Get paid. Go home."*
> Unknown

When we happen to know our colleague's remuneration, whether it is higher or lower than our expectations, it changes our perception and value of them; we now have a comparable scale to determine if one is overpaid or underpaid. Depending on which end of the scale we end up in this situation, we could feel encouraged or dismayed. If we are only comparing to a pure colleague, then that is all it is. We only have to deal with this 9 to 5. We say goodbye and go home and that is it, or at most, we go home and whinge about it. However, if our colleague is our friend or the friend has become our colleague, it does not matter which one comes first, then resentment remains after work, because the friendship surpasses the 9 to 5 time frame. That kind of friendship will become difficult to sustain. There is a two fold explanation for this. First, the cause is obvious, envy. Envy is part of human emotion as well as an instinct. Second, we only compare ourselves to the ones who are like us. Therefore avoid this situation at all costs.

The late Ayrton Senna had the wisdom to do so when teamed up with "the Professor" Alain Prost during the 1988-1989 seasons. The Brazilian legend, arguably one of the fastest Formula One drivers, did not start a relationship with Prost during their tenure together at McLaren. Senna purposely kept his distance from Prost. Though they were never friends to begin with, Senna did not see the need to start a friendship when they were immediate competitors. He was strictly professional and business-oriented, with no other strings attached, so he could solely focus on beating the driver with whom he shared the same garage. It might sound extreme, but that was what it took to achieve greatness in the golden era of Formula One. Senna was a beast and, rightly so, Senna made the wise decision.

Partnering with a Close One

Growing up, I have heard way too many stories about business partnerships or ventures between friends that went south when their true colours were revealed. I have been warned when opportunities arise, think twice when choosing business or friendship. You simply cannot have it both ways, it is always an either-or dilemma. There is no such thing as a friendly business; mixing friendship and business together is like pouring water into a pot of boiling oil. Just an analogy, please do not try this at home. Again, the scotoma here is that we often want to believe friendships translate to business compatibility and undermine the risk of offset values. People can be easy to hang out with but not necessarily easy to work with. Couples can spark during dating or courtship but that does not prove they are perfect for each other within the vows of marriage. Roles can be easily obscured and it won't be in the best interests of the business. Just remember, no matter how attractive the business may present on the table, if you see your friend on the other side of the table, ask yourself, do you have the courage to go ahead with the mindset of losing your mate, risking a friendship over potential monetary gain?

Back to the world of Formula One, the 2015 United States Grand Prix was one of the most watched races with 96.1 million tuning in to watch the championship unfold. The cap-gate also revealed in front of the global audience the unpleasant side of the two teammates who used to be friends. Hamilton and Rosberg are not the only pair who have turned from friends to foes; they are the most recent but surely not the last to burn their bridges. On the current 2020 grid, Frenchman Esteban Ocon of the Renault Formula One Team and fellow countryman Pierre Gasly of the Scuderia AlphaTauri were good friends growing up; no surprise, they do not talk anymore. In a recent interview, Rosberg said he could hopefully rekindle their friendship in the future when Formula One is in the past, while Hamilton expressed his idea of documenting all the behind the scene stories in his book after retirement. Will their friendship be able to travel back in time? Only time will tell.

"Winning has a price."
Michael Jordan

FUN FACTS ON UNITED STATES GRAND PRIX

Generally speaking, Americans are not fond of Formula One racing, after all, it was a sport coined by the British. Americans are proud of their own motor racing categories, namely Indy500 and Daytona; Formula One just did not come with a familiar accent for the Yankees. Having said that, Formula One still made it to the shores of the United States 49 times in 10 different locations in the 70-year span. Two of the recent circuits that hosted the event are the Indianapolis Motor Speedway (200-2007) and Circuit of the Americas in Austin, Texas (2012-current). The former, Indianapolis Motor Speedway, is known for the farce that raged across the Americas in 2005. The Grand Prix saw 14 Michelin cars ditching the race after the formation lap, leaving only 6 Bridgestone cars to fight it out. The Michelin cars had concerns over safety measures that their tyres were not sustainable through stress caused by the banker's corners at turn 13. No compromise had been reached between the teams and FIA, hence the opting out. The popularity of the sport took a plunge thereafter and is still in the process of surging back to compete with the local motor racing series.

WATCH

2014 Abu Dhabi Grand Prix, 2015 United States Grand Prix, 2016 Abu Dhabi Grand Prix.

DID YOU KNOW

Nico Rosberg's nickname among the fellow drivers is called Britney? This refers to his similarity in looks and blonde hair to the pop star diva Britney Spears.

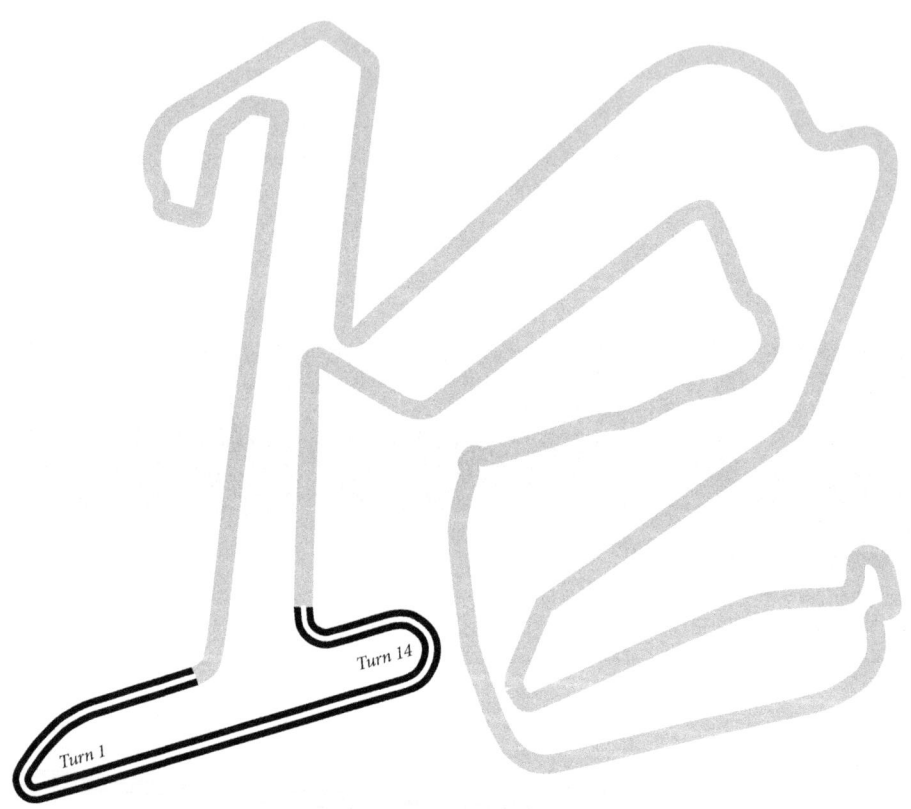

Hungaroring

47.582066186586545, 19.25060365850775

RACE 11

2019 Hungarian Grand Prix

70 Laps

*"And James, sorry I doubted that strategy.
That was a tall mountain."*

The Penultimate Race

My Formula One journey took off in 2006, and I considered it a good time to get into the sport because of the competitive nature of the grid during that stretch of the competition. Prior to 2006, It had been the Ferrari dynasty, dominated by the great Michael Schumacher, winning five drivers' titles and helping his Italian squad to bag equally prized constructors' championships. The second half of the 2000s had shifted its balance and been made more entertaining with the rise of Renault, McLaren and Brawn all taking their share of championship glories. All in all, it had produced five champion drivers in Schumacher, Fernando Alonso, Kimi Räikkönen, Lewis Hamilton and Jensen Button.

In the 2010s era though, it was considered dull and less competitive, to say the least. It was an era in history, that produced the most dead rubber[1] races (14). This 10-year span was dominated by two teams of three drivers compared to the four teams of five drivers in the 2000s. Sebastian Vettel won his four championships from 2010 to 2013 with Renault-powered Red

---

1 Dead rubber are the races where both constructors' and drivers' titles were already decided.

Bull Racing; the team collected 41 race victories of the possible 58 Grand Prix entries. From 2014 to 2019, the hybrid-powered era, Mercedes was simply untouchable and enthroned as serial winners; while their Italian rival from Maranello had produced competitive packages, their team often botched up with pit work and questionable strategic calls to let down their drivers. In historical context, Ferrari during this stretch was nothing more than mediocrity. That allowed the German constructors to take home six drivers' and six constructors' titles in succession, putting the rest to shame. The only consolation from the second half of the 2010s was probably the intensive rivalry between Hamilton and Rosberg. It goes without saying, once Rosberg decided to hang up his crash helmet after winning the 2016's drivers' title, the world championship was Hamilton's to lose from that point onwards. Do not get me wrong, Valtteri Bottas, the Finnish driver who replaced Rosberg after his shocking retirement, was a decent driver, but he was not world champion material, in my book.

2019 was the premonition of a changing of the guard; with the promotion of Monégasque Charles Leclerc, Ferrari was no longer Vettel's team. Max Verstappen, the sole Dutch hopeful, was officially Red Bull's number 1 driver after the departure of fan favourite Daniel Ricciardo. Both drivers, considerably young and quick, challenged Hamilton from race to race in 2019, and clearly, it was a matter of time for one of these two millennials to dethrone Hamilton from 2020 and beyond. Not to mention three other rookies by the names of Lando Norris, Alex Albon and George Russell, who joined the ranks and were marketed to bring a breath of fresh air to Formula One and its future.

Coming off from his second win of the season in a wet and wild German Grand Prix, a race widely received as the race of the decade, Verstappen arrived in Hungary full of confidence and hunger for more before the summer break. The 2019 Hungarian Grand Prix was the 12th of the 21 races, scheduled at the midway point in early August. 2019 had been the longest season to date and, for some drivers, the summer break could not come quickly enough. Not for Verstappen; the young Dutchman was just ready to peak. He claimed pole position on Saturday by just two-thousandth of a second over Bottas. This feat allowed him to become the first-ever Dutchman to secure pole position, and the 100th pole sitter for Formula One, adding another milestone to his achievement as the youngest driver to score world championship points (17 years, 180 days) and youngest race winner (18 years and 228 days). The young star had come a long way with his maturity in his race craft and on-track antics and was ready to shift into the next gear against the almighty Mercedes team.

On Sunday 4th August 2019, sky clear and sunny, all 20 cars took their spots on the grid. Verstappen had clean air in his sight with pole position, followed by the two silver arrows of Bottas and Hamilton. The two Ferraris, Leclerc and Vettel were only the third fastest team from the day before, they lined up P4 and P5. Verstappen's teammate Pierre Gasly found himself down at P6 in front of the two McLarens in Norris and Carlos Sainz Jr. The 1.6 litre V6 turbocharged engines were riotous ahead of the 70-lap race on a 4.83 km track with 14 corners, known as the Hungaroring.

Lights out and off they went. Verstappen, with a clean start, was followed closely behind by Hamilton, while Bottas botched his launch and tried to make up for his delayed reaction. The Finn tried staying side by side with his British teammate but locked up his front left steering into turn 1. Hamilton yielded to let Bottas but quickly swung back to his right, heading into turn 3 from the outside. Under pressure, Bottas locked up once again and this time Hamilton capitalised and had passed him by turn 3. Leclerc saw the vulnerable Finn, took the advantage and moved alongside him and slightly shoved the Mercedes aside. The replay showed Leclerc's Ferrari was too close to Bottas for comfort and the Mercedes driver lost parts of his end plates[2] from the scuffle; a costly scrimmage that forced Bottas to pit for new front wings and dropped him back to the tail by lap 6.

2 End plates are the sides that hold the front wings. It is an integral design to the front wing to bring aero-efficiency to the car.

Verstappen benefited from the fight and enjoyed clean air together with Hamilton not too far behind. By lap 13, the pair started to break away from the rest by a margin of 10 seconds, while the two Ferraris behind segregated themselves from the midfielders. The race settled when heading into the first pit stop window, as predicted by the pundits; a one-stop strategy was the optimum on this circuit. Red Bull made the first move by getting race leader Verstappen to pit on lap 25 and serve his mandatory switch to hard compound rubber. Since it was Verstappen pitting first, Hamilton and his team did not have a choice to undercut, hence Hamilton was instructed to attempt an overcut instead. It was ambitious, as the gap was too big to close. Hamilton's tyres lasted 7 laps further than his immediate rival, and he pitted for fresh hard at lap 32 to set him up for another go at Verstappen.

Pumping out faster laps and closing in on the Dutchmen, Hamilton was close enough when the two crossed the start-finish line to begin their 39th lap. The British champion saw his opportunity when both drivers had to clear the backmarker[3] in Ricciardo of Renault. Hamilton fancied his chances, going outside with late braking into turn 1. Verstappen had better traction and exit speed to keep his position but Hamilton powered his Mercedes alongside the Red Bull, going wheel to wheel into turn 2, Verstappen again benefited from the inside line, keeping his position. Come turn 4, Hamilton again chose to go outside, but went wide into the run-off area, coming off second best from the battle. It was some battle; both drivers drove brilliantly to defend and attack with respect. Verstappen gave the reigning world champion a run for his money. I was on the edge of my seat, and seeking for more.

However, Hamilton's F1 W10 began to struggle with brake issues, overheating from the dirty air[4] of Verstappen's RB15. He was significantly

---

3 Backmarker refers to a driver at the rear end of the field, they will be shown a blue flag to give way to the race leaders before being lapped.

4 Dirty air refers to the turbulence air a car is receiving when getting too close to the car in front through corners. Not to be mistaken by slipstream in a straight line, dirty air can cause overheating in both the tyres and engines and also understeer or oversteer when the downforce setup is compromised.

slower in corners, speculating he was lifting and coasting[5] through the corners to cool his brakes.

"What more can I do man?" Hamilton was helpless as he pleaded his situation to his race engineer on the radio.

"Just keep the pressure on, once you got the temps up…" Peter Bonnington, also known as Bono, Hamilton's race engineer gave his advice from the pit wall.

"I can't keep the pressure on," Hamilton again defended his situation.

Verstappen was momentarily excused from the fight, as round 1 seemed to conclude for the time being with the advantage going to the Dutchman. Still about 1.2 seconds behind the race leader on lap 48, Mercedes needed some head-scratching to relieve their number 1 driver. Hungaroring has a reputation for being extremely difficult to overtake on, and the team was rallying to put their driver ahead amidst of all the on-track effort. James Vowles, chief strategist for the German outfit, made a bold chess move and pitted Hamilton for a new set of medium Pirellis. It was a strategic call, nobody saw it coming, as the frontrunners were expected to do a one-stop race. There was method in Mercedes's madness because it was rational to pit Hamilton at that time; since they could not gain any ground on track, they might as well try to beat them by throwing caution to the wind. After all, people in this business believe that fortune favours the bold.

"I don't know if that was the right call man." Hamilton questioned as he exited the pit.

"Copy that Lewis, I think you've got the pace." Bono assured him.

"And how far away is he now?" Hamilton asked.

---

5 Lifting and coasting is an adaptation in driving when drivers need to save fuel and he will use fewer throttles by lifting throttle earlier when approaching corners and coasting through. Sometimes the driver needs to lift and coast because of mechanical issues with gears.

"Verstappen 19 seconds ahead." Bono related the answer back to his driver.

Hamilton had his doubts about the strategy; perhaps the incident months earlier in the Monaco Grand Prix was still fresh from his memory. In that race, Mercedes pitted Hamilton on medium tyres during a safety car intervention on lap 11, and expected him to drive with them to the chequered flag, while rival Max Verstappen was on hard compound. Hamilton started to struggle with his tyres from lap 20 and had to endure the 72-lap race with Verstappen hunting behind with better grip. It was a happy ending for the British champion, crossing the line first despite driving with dead tyres for the last 20 laps and fending off a faster Red Bull. He drove brilliantly, and the team strategists were let off the hook with their questionable call.

In Hungary's race, the pit stop did not compromise track position, as Hamilton had enough lead over the third-placed Leclerc. What was lost was the track time from pitting for tyres, approximately 20 seconds. In Red Bull's point of view, if they reacted to Mercedes, there was a higher probability that Verstappen might lose the lead to Hamilton, as the pit time was too close for comfort. The Austrian team opted to stay with their plan A of one-stop in the hope they could make it to the chequered flag before Hamilton's fightback on the new rubber. 20 seconds in 20 laps; the five-time world champion needed to push his car faster than the man who was leading the race by more than one second per lap. It was Hammertime[6]!

Doing what he does best, visor down and qualifying mode on, Hamilton was relishing his speed to meet the target after struggling early with the cold tyres. Driving flat out, lap by lap he was catching up to Verstappen and chiselling away the Dutchman's lead. By lap 66, the Red Bull's rubber was tailing off, due to ageing and minimal grip, while Hamilton was in his gearbox ready to pounce. DRS opened, Hamilton floored the throttle,

---

6 Hammertime is a radio message code Hamilton's engineer implied to ask Hamilton to push and do an all-out lap.

made his move on the outside again and passed by Verstappen; this time with ease with just a few laps to spare. Red Bull quickly accepted defeat and pitted their number 1 driver for a new set of medium tyres to contest for fastest lap honour[7] and salvage an extra championship point, since the race victory was not possible. Hamilton flexed his muscles and piloted his Mercedes home, his 8th race victory of the season, 81st of his career, 10 short of equalling Michael Schumacher's all-time record race wins.

"Well done mate, that was an incredible drive!" the team sent congratulatory messages through the radio.

"And James, sorry I doubted that strategy. It was a tall mountain, but grateful we did it." Hamilton thanked his team.

Life Lesson #11
Teamwork makes the Dream Work

The Hungarian race was won on merit, based on a bold strategic call. As a driver, Hamilton paid his dues and his team rewarded him with the right tools to fight for the victory. As much as Hamilton doubted the calls in his cockpit, he needed to trust the team's decision and live with the outcome. Formula One is a misleading sport; it portrays drivers as the stars of the show, and occasionally highlights the team bosses as the sidekicks, and undermines the crew who work behind the scenes. Formula One without a doubt is a team sport, in both the way it structures the competition and the reward system. Two drivers from each constructor enter the Grand Prix weekend and compete for themselves and also on behalf of their team. The same amount of championship points the drivers earn will also go

7 Since 2019, fastest lap will be awarded an extra championship point providing the driver finishes in top 10 in final race classification. This provides an additional dimension to the competition and encourages drivers to fight for the honour.

toward the team's tally in their constructor's bid for the championship. In a nutshell, Formula One season is about who is the best driver and who is the best constructor.

By now we know that Formula One cars are complex machines and no one person can tame such a beast all by themselves. Everything in this sport is measured and quantified. The mechanics piece together 25,000 parts to create the work of art and tune the car to perfection with inch-perfect angles and dials. Every bit counts towards success, every part needs to earn its place on the bodywork of the car. A $50.00 part from the car could make the difference between hero or zero in their title fight, according to James Allison, chief designer of Mercedes.

The engineers work day and night to crunch the numbers and map out parameters through the telemetries gathered from 120 sensors installed on the car. For your information, during a race, each car sends out 750 million numbers according to Peter Van Manen's TedTalk in 2013. Every piece of information is recorded, analysed, decoded and translated into literacy and numeracy; 0.01 second is equivalent to 10cm on tack, 1kg from the driver can cost up to 0.03 seconds difference per lap so on and so forth. It fully requires a team of various experts to work on and off the track to deliver performance and results.

In Hungary, Mercedes's strategists were the catalyst behind the win in the eyes of the broadcasters, and perhaps the viewer like myself, but let us not forget the pit crew also were very much on their games for their parts in the race. Not to mention the same pit crew that worked on the car as mechanics in assembling and tuning the car for practice and qualifying sessions. Off-site, a team of a dozen engineers working in what they called a mission control room in their factory, oversee data analysis live during the race to generate feedback that potentially allows the team to decide on the race plans; they are the unsung heroes. This, like any other win by any other car or driver, is nowhere near a one-man show. No one driver can do it alone, it is always a team effort. The desire to win is not reserved for an individual driver, it is shared among hundreds of co-workers. The genuine excitement is always evident in the post-race ceremony when the team flocks beneath the rostrum.

Grease Monkeys in the Garage

The pit crew is very much part of the show in the modern Grand Prix weekend, especially after the omission of refuelling in 2010. A 20-man pit crew can often be the hero or zero, having as much impact on the race as the driver. A simple mistake can easily cast the entire race weekend into ground zero. The front jack man that stops the car, then together with the rear jack man raises the car in the air, all in about 0.3 second. Two tyre carriers for each wheel, one to pull them off and the other to put on the new set. One gunman from each corner with the pneumatic gun to first loosen then tighten the wheel nut whilst the carriers perform the switch. Two mechanics stabilize the car while work is carried out. Two more mechanics at the front to tend to the front wings to either clear debris or adjust wing angle. One mechanic at the rear to look out for the pit lane traffic, and one to standby with a fire extinguisher in case of fire. All need to be completed in perfect harmony with absolute precision in just under 3 seconds. Anything more, they will be jeopardising track position and race outcome. The team's contribution determines much of the success of an individual driver, it can be a make or break a relationship from race to race or season to season. Red Bull's staggering 1.82-second pit stop in Brazil 2019 still remains as the world record for the fastest tyre change work.

If you did not think that was impressive enough, in the 2012 Indian Grand Prix, McLaren's pit crew helped their then-driver Lewis Hamilton to change five wheels in a 3.3 seconds turnaround; that was changing the four Pirelli tyres plus swapping his steering wheel all at the same time. Apparently, Hamilton had issues with shift paddles and had to compromise his driving. The team made the call to pit for new tyres while also replacing his malfunctioning steering wheel. Hamilton needed to shift the car to neutral, release the steering wheel, lock in the new one and put it in gear again, all in the space of 3 seconds while his car was lifted up for tyre change. Google the footage and it will impress you how incredibly fast and seamless they were. If that does not impress you, I don't know what will!

The world has evolved and segregated people's talent into more refined specialisations. Though the current education system was built upon the foundation of producing workers for the 20th century, we have slowly developed a new curriculum to fit the needs of the 21st century. Areas of specialisation have been expanded; what used to be just a team of 12 men to construct a Formula One car in the 70s has grown to a team of hundreds, each paying distinctive attention to make the car talk.

> ## "We don't have to do all of it alone. We were never meant to."
> Brene Brown

The Chopsticks Analogy

In many aspects of our life, we do not work alone either; work or family life. We do not and we should not, if we are after great results. We are in the age of collaboration and are far from the days where we put all our eggs in one basket. A person's capability is limited, a team's capability is limitless. Take a disposable chopstick and try to snap it in half; it should be a piece of cake for most grown adults. Try doing the same with a bunch of them together and it would almost be physically impossible unless you are David Horne. This comes from a famous Chinese analogy that I learned growing up, similar to the African proverb in "Sticks in a bundle are unbreakable". It taught me the importance of teamwork and the power of multiplying. A lone wolf is a thing of a past when we are recognised diversity and surrounded by talent and experts in all disciplines. We need to make a judgement on making good use of people around us to get ahead of our own game.

Show gratitude and appreciation to our team and teammates in life, our spouse or partner. Because of their input in our ecology, that may be left unnoticed. Things like re-washing the dishes for us without letting us know, or picking up crumbs from the floor after we eat. We might think these are a tiny little peanut in life, but it is those little insignificant events that make a difference on a racing track. Every little detail counts towards the success, quality or the degree happiness of our life. Take them out of the equation, we can become a venerable soul. My tip is, be generous with our gratitude toward those who surround us, those people who we call team. Appreciate their presence in good times and bad times, because it is those people who make us a champion in life.

"Great things are done by a series of small things brought together."

Vincent Van Gogh

Talent is Never Enough on Its Own

The recent Netflix documentary titled "The Last Dance" compiled much-unseen footage recorded during Michael Jordan's career with the Chicago Bulls and their incredible title runs during the 90s. The documentary uncovered as many closed-door affairs, such as Jordan's belief in teamwork. As unstoppable as Jordan was in his prime, he understood clearly he needed to win in combination with all 11 teammates. Not just the starting five players who shared the court, but also all the players coming off the bench were equally important. He cultivated a winning culture, leading by example and constantly motivating and challenging his teammates on and off the court. He had to build trust and rapport through some hard lessons with star calibre players as well as players who played only 10 to 15 minutes a night.

Jordan and Steve Kerr's relationship was well documented in this 10 episode series. The pair had gained each other's trust via an altercation in one of the team's scrimmages. That trust was put to the test in the closing minute in game six of the 1997 NBA Final against Utah Jazz. With 28 seconds left on the game clock and the ball game tied at 86-86 with the championship on the line, all eyes were on Jordan, the GOAT. During the timeout, Jordan foresaw what was coming from Utah's defence and told Kerr to be ready to take the final shot; true enough, that was exactly how it unfolded. Utah sent two players to double team Jordan as the clock wind down. Jordan, as he had planned in his head, got the ball to Kerr at the exact moment for an open jumper. Kerr drilled the 15-footer, a game-winner and sealed their fifth title in seven years.

On the biggest stage, the clutch moment that was designed for greatness like himself, he made a wise decision to look for an open shot from his teammate. He did not force a shot up or play hero ball, he played a team game. He never did it all by himself, he played off his game with his teammates. That was what made Jordan greater than the rest.

"Talent wins games, but teamwork and intelligence win championships."
Michael Jordan

Teamwork involves understanding each other's strengths and weakness and working with a common goal to motivate one another; building trust by delegating loads to specific departments, co-workers and team members for efficiency output. Beware not to bite off more than we can chew. Delegation is the key to any success in teamwork; sharing ideas and thoughts to problem solve as a collective group to expand the capacity and empower the team. Long gone are the days of individualism; embrace the era of collaboration and team spirit.

The Crossover Perspective

We live in an era of collaboration, and it has become more apparent in the digital era where demand from the consumer market is growing rapidly. Brands new and old are seeking new ways to expand their market share within a competitive and saturated consumer market. While consumers are smart buyers, brands need to constantly create trends that connect. Collaboration from brands has become a strategy employed by some of the big names from Nike and Apple, Spotify and Uber to GoPro and Red Bull to name a few. These partnerships, along with many others, allow both brands to tap into each other's existing customer base and resources without investing more than they need to; a win-win situation where both brands can instantly leverage returns, and this type of cross collaboration is well received in the digital realm. Collaboration by Youtubers is very common for the sole purpose of expanding viewers and subscribers from each other. It is indeed an era to celebrate diversity and embrace working with others.

Under Toto Wolff, team Mercedes has been kept under a tight ship for their successful dynasty since 2014. Apart from some tension in managing two talented drivers in Hamilton and Rosberg in their earlier stretch, they can consider themselves one of the dominant constructors in Formula One history. As gifted as he may be, the six-time world champion Hamilton would not have won without a strong team like Mercedes, and Hamilton owes his success to Niki Lauda who was the man who lured him from McLaren and was an integral part of the team and its success.

The Economist, an international weekly newspaper, published a mathematical model, developed from a study by Andrew Bell of the University of Sheffield. The study provides a statistical analysis of the relative importance of teams and drivers in a successful campaign. Considering team, driver and other factors that contribute to the championship points earned, it clearly demonstrated that, during a five-year span, the team was responsible for an average of 40% of track success, while Hamilton contributed 20% to his championship aspiration. The team and the car had a significant share of the success.

In retrospective, Hamilton did not win with the team overnight, even considering the fact that he won the title in his second year with the Woking team. Their partnerships needed teething periods and to develop chemistry along the way. He had to trust the team and live with the result because, in sports, you win and lose as a team. Giving credit where credit is due, Hamilton is on par to break the great Michael Schumacher's all-time record in race victories at 91. He could not have, or would not have done it without his team. Teamwork makes the dream work. Let us celebrate this idea by surrounding ourselves with great teammates at work, at home and in a social context; they are the ones that will take us and our lives to the next level.

"F1 is a team sport, not an individual sport."
Lance Stroll

FUN FACTS ON TEAMWORK

Red Bull has always been an efficient team known for its record-breaking tyre change. In the 2020 Hungarian Grand Prix, Max Verstappen had an embarrassing moment during his outlap before the race. The crash at turn 12 damaged his car, jeopardizing his race entry. The mechanics put on a show in front of the global audience, fixing the Red Bull while it was parked on the grid with all the pre-race activities and distraction happening in the background. Racing against the clock, the mechanics pulled off the feat and allowed their driver to do the rest. Verstappen, in return, rewarded the team with a P2 performance. At the other end of the spectrum, teams can easily throw their drivers in at the deep end, namely Ferrari during the Vettel era. When they say a team can throw a spanner in the works, they literally can. In the 1998 Italian Grand Prix, a Sauber mechanic mistakenly left a spanner in Johnny Herbert's C31 cockpit. The spanner got in the way of the brake pedal on lap 13 when Herbert struggled to brake heading into turn 7 and beached at the second Lesmo. A similar blunder happened to Renault's Robert Kubica in the 2010 Bahrain Grand Prix; a mechanic left his phone inside the Polo's cockpit, forcing him to pit and return the device.

WATCH

2019 Hungarian Grand Prix, 2019 Monaco Grand Prix.

DID YOU KNOW

Lewis Hamilton became the first and only Formula One champion of British and African descent when he won the driver's title with McLaren in 2008?

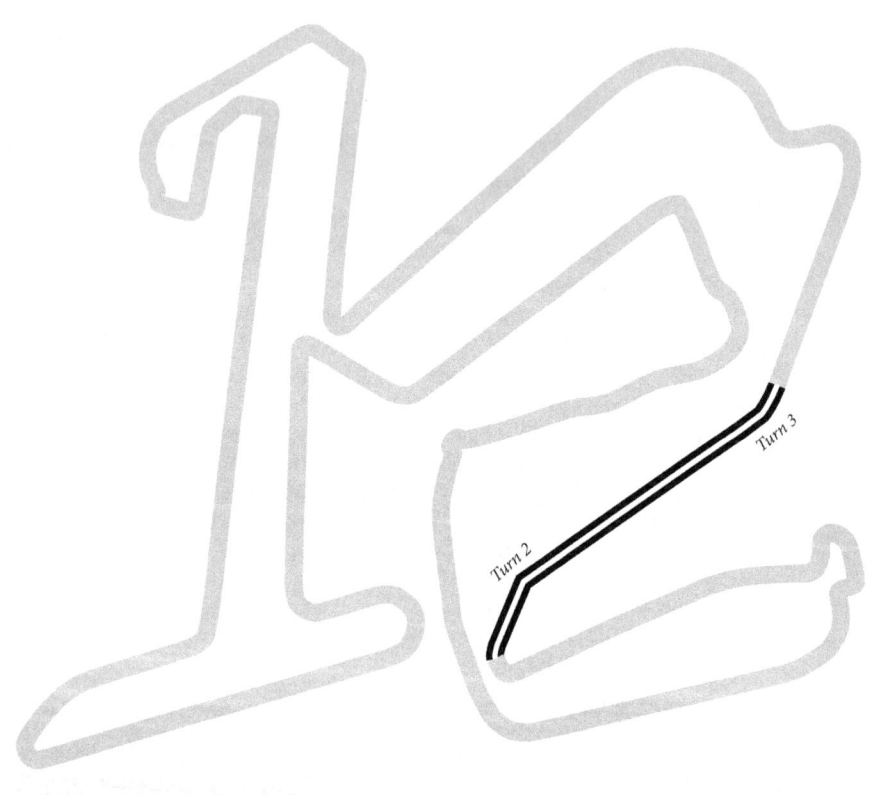

Fuji International Speedway

35.37243469930496, 138.9272934975155

RACE 12

1976 Japanese Grand Prix

73 Laps

"It was only when I realised this was what dying was that I shook it off and tried to wake up."

Do or Die

This book started by looking at the racing scene in the 1970s, and I thought it would only be fitting to come full circle and conclude the book with a race in the same era in this chapter. 1976, the year Niki Lauda and James Hunt went toe to toe with many dramas unfolding in between. A bit of a history lesson in many ways, as the season occurred a few years before my existence. 1976 proved to be the year that was significant to the names of Lauda and Hunt, hence it was difficult in my opinion to leave the two legends out of this affair of mine. The more I studied the season, the more I was fascinated about the accounts. If you are an experienced Formula One fan, you already know where this is heading.

It was an era where the pinnacle of motorsport was not considered, but in actual fact, an unimaginably dangerous and deadly sport. In the 70s, with an unacceptable and insane mortality rate by today's standards, the sport claimed 19 lives. Safety was paramount as far as drivers were concerned, but innovation for safety measures just could not come fast enough. Racing and death are almost like part and parcel of the deal drivers sign up for. British champion Sir Jackie Stewart explained racing in the 60s and 70s had to accept not just the possibility but the probability of dying each time they climbed into the cockpit. With that in mind, those years produced some of the bravest pilots and frightening races in Formula One history.

> *"Why did I look in my rear-view mirror every time I left home to race and wonder whether I would see it again?"*
>
> Sir Jackie Stewart

The year started with Lauda and Hunt squaring off as an equally competitive adversaries. Lauda, the reigning world champion was behind the wheel for the mighty Ferrari, just the third year into his contract with the Italian squad. After spending his first three years of his Formula One career in second-rate machines with the new Hesketh Racing, self-funded by Lord Hesketh, Hunt finally got his break to race with the big team, Marlboro Team McLaren. Hunt was thrown a lifeline after Hesketh ran out of money to keep a team around him, and McLaren needed a driver to fill Emerson Fittipaldi's departure; Hunt knew this was the chance of a lifetime. You could say, after a couple of years of battle, the duo could finally compete on almost equal terms in the big league.

For the calculating Austrian, Lauda's campaign started where he left off, finishing in front and winning. He was clearly the driver to beat, victorious in four of the first six Grand Prix and finishing on the podium every single time for the first nine races, with the exception of his sole retirement in France. For the charismatic Brit, Hunt kick-started his McLaren career in a less spectacular fashion, retiring four out of his first six races. As a consolation though, he claimed his maiden victory in Spain in controversial turmoil, before winning his second race in France in more convincing manner. All was still to play for when the season approached the second half, with Lauda leading the world championship by 20 points[1].

Then came the German Grand Prix.

The 1976 German Grand Prix took place in notorious Nürburgring, a traditional circuit noted for its long and technical characteristics. It had changed quite a bit over the years, but in 1976 the track layout was a long gruelling 22.8km challenge. Lauda, the record holder for the old layout at Nürburgring, objected to taking part, with the pre-race weather being unkind. He was concerned with the track conditions and the safety management on-site posing threats to all peers, and pleaded his case during the drivers' meeting. His view was not widely received at the time and the drivers voted to go ahead, leaving Lauda with no choice but to fulfil his contractual obligation.

In retrospective, Lauda was right; conditions at the beginning of the race were putting drivers' safety in jeopardy. It did not take long for anyone to realise that. Just two laps into the race, a spectator with a 8mm recorder captured Lauda coming off the right-hander and lost his Ferrari, hammered into the barriers and pinballing, engulfed in flames in a blink and collecting Brett Lunger's Surtees in the process. The Ferrari champion was a sitting duck in an 800-degree inferno for a minute too long before he was rescued by his peers; a horrific accident that could have easily taken his life instantaneously. Lauda was helicoptered to the nearest hospital with severe burns on his face and body and lapsed into a coma. The Austrian driver flirted with death and miraculously survived and returned to the track just six weeks after the near-fatal accident to defend his title. He was not expected to live, yet his determination sparked his recovery and overcame his physical and mental state.

---

1 The championship point scoring system in 1976 awarded only the top 6 finishers. With the winner receiving 9 points, then 6, 4, 3, 2, 1 for the remaining 5 drivers. 20 points would be equivalent to more than two race wins.

"It was only when I realised this was what dying was that I shook it off and tried to wake up," said Niki Lauda, remembering how he had confronted death.

His sheer will power and determination had overcome any pain caused by the accident, physically and mentally. Lauda, in his autobiography "To Hell and Back" shared his experience and thoughts while recovering in the hospital. With the absence of Lauda, Hunt was banking points and catching up on the leader board; that was enough to serve as the sole motivation to will Lauda back behind the wheels in just six weeks. Missing two Grand Prix, he returned to the pit lane for the Italian Grand Prix to continue his battle with Hunt. He put on his game face and hid his fear under his crash helmet. In his own words, Lauda was frightened, but he knew he could not afford to show any of that to his rival. He refused to surrender, and forced his way to the grid. He battled on and finished in P4 with an incredible performance, a result that surprised everyone including the pundits.

Nothing could describe Lauda's fighting spirit, on and off track, to carry on his campaign against Hunt, which draws our attention to the conclusion of the season at Fuji; the Japanese Grand Prix, host of the season finale in 1976. A fitting closure for the dramatic season that saw Lauda and Hunt battling to be the last man standing. Arriving in the land of the rising sun, the Austrian defending champion had a 3-point lead over his English rival; he would keep his title if he finished in front or finished behind Hunt with no more than one place in between. For Hunt, his championship permutations were to win the race or finish in the top four, with Lauda finishing two to three places behind. It was still everyone's race to win or lose.

On Sunday 24th October 1976, just like many season finales in Formula One's history, the heavens opened and the rain came to show its support. The rain arrived not to shower on anyone's parade, rather, challenging them to rise to the occasion and show their champion aspirations. The rain was tempestuous, to say the least, and had drivers and event organiser's fidgeting with nerves. Drivers were concerned but, due to contractual obligations, the organiser decided to persist with the race in the treacherous conditions. The recorded race I watched 40 years later in a 4:3 ratio had a primitive quality when it comes to screen resolution. The experience was unique and, if I had to put it into words, then it was really like watching a high definition race without my glasses. The rain spitting down like cats and dogs did not help either. No aids from the screen in terms of lap counts, leaders, intervals or lap time of any sort. The race was followed and comprehended based on the commentary alone. Nevertheless, the experience was, let's say, one of its kind for my liking.

Despite all the lenses pointing towards Lauda and Hunt, the star of the show was an American by the name of Mario Andretti in Lotus, who secured pole position before Hunt and Lauda, leaving the two title contenders in P2 and P3 respectively. When the race went underway, Andretti had an indecisive start, letting Hunt by with ease just metres off the starting line on woefully lubricated asphalt. The American was soon passed by John Watson of Penske for P2 before they slowed down to ease into turn 1. Hunt drew first blood, and he intended to stay there to capture his major trophy. The mist in the air, together with the clouds of spray from the cars, made it extremely difficult to watch the race from TV. It is hard to imagine how the drivers were coping with such appalling conditions and staying on the track. Hunt benefited from the lead with clear air and pulled out a good solid lead after lap 1, while Lauda dropped to P5, perhaps waiting for the race to come to him by track conditions. The TV camera never captured where Lauda was due to the spray, and his position was only confirmed by the commentary. While Hunt was leading comfortably at the front, Andretti moved up to P2 and the next thing we saw was Lauda's Ferrari pitting.

The Ferrari 312T2 was stationary for an extended period of time while no physical work was conducted on the car. Communication took place between Lauda and his team before the Austrian removed himself from the cockpit. For what reason, nobody watching TV knew at the time. The commentator had no answers and assumed now that the championship was in the hands of Hunt. The Brit did what he needed to do for a good 60 laps before the track condition dried up as his tyres wore down. Patrick Depailler of the six-wheeled Tyrell[2] made an inside move, passing Hunt for the lead on lap 62 or thereabouts. Hunt was visibly struggling for grip and his tyres were crying for help just as Andretti charged passed him for P2 in his black and gold Lotus, then a few corners later pulled a move over Depailler for the lead.

With only five laps remaining and the championship on the line, Lauda's teammate Clay Regazzoni was chasing Hunt for P3; if Hunt was demoted, he would not win the title. He and the McLaren team could not accept the status quo and rolled the dice with Hunt as his M23 crippled into the pit lane. His tyres were flat and dead; I mean literally dead. The British team took a long 27 seconds before relieving Hunt for a free run to the chequered flag. It was now or never, and the 27-year-old star soldiered on; with only four laps to go and a couple of positions to make up, it was a huge task. Hunt was in his tunnel vision, driving on the limit with pure instinct and skill on a damp surface, but he held his nerve and made up the lost time corner after corner. It was qualifying lap performance to the flag, something he must have viusalised many times. Having sighted a pair of cars in front, Hunt gathered his composure, and with a ball of steel, pulled off two stunning moves over Regazzoni then Alan Jones of Surtees to secure the point he needed. He held it together and crossed the flag in P3 to win his first and only world title by the skin of his teeth; a single point over Lauda.

This rivalry between Lauda and Hunt was a significant part of Formula One history. It has been well documented in various forms and shapes,

---

2 The Tyrrell P34 was a six-wheeled challenger competed during the 1976 season. The radical design raised eyebrows from its competitors, however, the concept was abandoned in 1978 together with new rules from F1 to stipulate cars to have only four wheels.

by both the professionals and the amateurs. I had watched video footage, interviews and read Lauda's biography before watching the race in full. This has made it less exciting knowing what would happen from lap to lap, nevertheless the glory of Hunt's race victory has in no way been diminished. The season finale did live up to its hype, for British fans at least.

Life Lesson #12

Pick your Battles

Lauda later confirmed to the media that he retired from the race on lap 2 voluntarily, based on safety grounds. The Nürburgring incident, still fresh in his memory, was looming in the background. He knew front and centre that he did not want to place himself in a similar situation after surveying race conditions for the two litmus test laps. The rational side of him prevailed and he picked his battle correctly; he did not need to fight this one out with his life. After knocking on heaven's door, he knew what was more important. Life or championship glory? The latter was immaterial, when danger was off the chart; it was an easy choice. He picked his battle.

"I always knew about the risks I was taking. Every year, someone you knew was killed racing. You had to ask yourself, do you enjoy driving these cars so much that you're prepared to take that risk?"

Niki Lauda

In life, we are confronted by challenges at every corner, every lap, every race and every season. We can put up a fight for everything that is thrown at us; sometimes we win, other times we concede. Yielding does not necessarily imply we are on the weaker side, in many ways, it can indicate otherwise. I never believed Lauda was weaker by withdrawing from the race, nor did I ever think he would lose had he chosen to carry on. The fact that he returned to the cockpit from a horrific injury, and raced with bloody wounds, showed more of his strength over his racing peers. He had a clear vision of what he was after, even with the adrenaline pumping, and he was able to make wise and conscious decisions. Life ranked higher than pursuing the championship.

My Battles to Pick

Growing up, I never saw myself as a difficult kid during the adolescent years, perhaps because my brother took up the role of the rebellious child in the family. The most damage I have caused my parents to pull their hair out was my reluctance to visit the hairdresser more often than not, and the ear-piercing I got when they specifically asked me not to. Otherwise, I was considered a teenager who was easy to parent. With this experience or lack thereof, I approached teenage parenthood with little expectation, or ignorance. Therefore it was extremely difficult to cope when my teenage daughter began to slam the door on me on occasions. It bothered me so much that I googled "how to deal with teens", and one of the returned results suggested to "remove all the doors in the house".

I did not take this advice for obvious reasons of privacy and humanity issues, especially in this day and age, not to mention that I am not a trained handyman to do the job. I had to seek an alternative apart from the almighty google. I ended up benefiting from professional counselling with a few tricks and planted some strategies in place. In the past, the door slamming had triggered my anger and forced me into further confrontation that led to an escalation of the situation; the problem only got worse and snowballed. I have since learned how to pick my battles. Slamming doors is something I am willing to yield to give each other more space and by taking one step backwards, I allowed myself to move two steps forwards later. This approach opened up my perspective on dealing with my emotions when it comes to making adequate decisions. What is worth fighting at the time and what is not.

As covered in an earlier chapter, the make-up of human nature wants to win by default, and that is a simple primal instinct. We fight to win, to survive, to feel the existence or be part of the community. The truth of the matter is, we cannot win all the battles we pick, or let me rephrase that, we cannot fight all the battles we encounter. There will be things in life we fight for and there will be things we choose to walk away from. Picking our battles is an undeniably important lesson that goes a long way. Being wise and calm helps us to weigh out the battle in front of us; the solution lies in choosing the one that is going to help us win the war. Having our sights set on the bigger picture and not clinging on to the small battles that may or may not come to fruition is essential to a successful life.

It sounds simple but is always tricky to implement when we are not able to think on our feet. Be conscious when choosing our battles, and that means to be selective of the problems, issues, confrontations that we face. Think strategically, do not make decisions lightly and let emotion get the better of us. Fight intelligently and thoughtfully or leave the battle to save our time and energy for something worthy. We should look before we leap.

Every fight, big or small, requires investing effort, energy and time. In any investment, be it financial, physical or mental, we need to envision the ROI, return of investment. Not all things in life can be, or should be calculated, or even digitised, but can serve as a guide for us to make good decisions. The return, equivalent to worthiness, perhaps should be the first question asked prior to any battle. Asking questions with such reverence could help stall the process by buying more time to think things over, rationally, making sure we are not finding a storm in a teacup.

Hunt was a world champion by merit and by character. Acting instinctively, he was willing to risk his life and limb, and everything in between, to win. He left nothing on the table and gave all he had and the rest was in the lap of God. He was a worthy champion without a doubt and he knew opportunity does not come by every year. The British loose canon raced as if it was his last. He came into the final race with the mentality of trying to win the title by all means, convincing himself and others around him that he would win or die trying. He chose his battle, and it paid off when he finally reached the summit.

As for Lauda, he made his own choices as well. He was highly intelligent, with his own clinical and philosophical approach to the final few races. By returning to fight for the title, followed by withdrawing in the championship-defying race, there was a lot of deep thinking involved. He did not want to throw in the towel without trying, just like Hunt. Unlike other drivers who think based on their bums, Lauda was thinking on his feet on this occasion. He had lived and learned his lesson from Nürburgring. He put himself out of the picture in Japan, and let Hunt work for the title. Win or lose, he came with no regret and no stone left unturned because he knew he had given more than anyone could have provided in that very circumstance.

Arguably, Lauda is the most courageous champion who has ever graced in Formula One tracks. He wanted more championship to his legacy, but he knew he needed a life that he could share those moments with. He took a step backwards in order to make two more moves forward later. He was proven right. Lauda took back his title the following season in 1977, winning his second world championship, then again in 1984, three years after his first retirement from the sport, to become a triple world champion for McLaren. Despite not winning the title in 1976, he has always been remembered as one of the greatest and the most courageous champions in Formula One history.

He achieved all these, by choice, a wise choice.

"My life is worth more than a title."
Niki Lauda

FUN FACTS ON NIKI LAUDA & JAMES HUNT

Lauda and Hunt had a healthy relationship during their racing careers. In their younger days, while competing in the junior categories in F3 and F2, the pair had shared more than just memories on the track; the Brit and the Austrian shared accommodation in Monaco for an extended period of time. The rivalry between the two familiar foes was mostly defined by the media, which, to their credit elevated the championship to another level. The distinctive styles of the two drivers provided much of the spotlight. The duo had great respect for one another as formidable opponents, despite the fact that the Hollywood movie "Rush", as mentioned in the first chapter, dramatised the rivalry for moviegoers. Hunt died at the age of 42 due to heart failure, while Lauda continued to serve as a great ambassador for Formula One until 2019 when he passed away suffering from kidney issues at the age of 70. The passing of the two legendary drivers speaks for itself in many ways. The unreserved Hunt with do or die mentality had his life cut short while the calculative Lauda lived on by his philosophy.

WATCH

1976 German Grand Prix, 1976 Italian Grand Prix, 1976 Japanese Grand Prix.

DID YOU KNOW

Niki Lauda once traded his collection of winner's trophies for a free lifetime car wash? He saw his silverware as nothing but metal scraps.

CHEQUERED FLAG

"...And so you touch this limit, something happens and you suddenly can go a little bit further."

The average male life expectancy in Australia is 82.5 years, according to The World Bank in 2017. Half that figure gives me 41.25 years, a number that resembles my age at the time of writing this sentence. In other words, I have reached the halfway mark of my life, so to speak, if I can at least make it to 82, fingers crossed. Reaching halfway and turning the corner for the second half of my life was a significant moment for me. I realised there are more birthdays behind me than there are in front of me. Overwhelming may be an overstatement, but I strongly felt compelled to express my life in a more profound manner.

The great 20th century psychologist Carl Gustav Jung once quoted by saying, *"Life begins at 40, and up until then you are just doing research."* This left me pondering what research I have done in my 40 years, and how I can transform this into a more meaningful form.

40 years is a long time to shape one's identity. I grew up having many aspirations from my older brother, shaping who I am with various personality traits, skill sets and interests. Being the typical youngest child in the family, I was easily influenced and would mirror anything my brother would do, from appreciation through the lens of creative art and design, passion for American sports, to the taste of rock and roll music. All became part of who I was as a person for the first 25 years of my life.

Then Formula One came knocking on my door.

It rocked my world and provided a brand new perspective on life; revolutionised me in many ways to realign my core values. It connects my life with philosophies and life lessons from race to race. To identify with Carl Jung's quote, I am happy to say that my greatest discovery in the first 40 years of my life would be my conviction to Formula One, religion aside. With this revelation, my life officially began at 40 with the idea of documenting and marrying Formula One with my life experiences.

So, with 14 years spending more than 1,000 adrenaline-pumping hours over 270 races (and counting), together with 11 months in the making and more than 200 relentless hours over 50,000 words over countless nights, I have reached a new plateau in life. Never would I have imagined myself writing something of this magnitude, after all, English is not my first language and writing has never been my bread and butter. Regardless of constant self-doubt and all the bumps along the way, during the unprecedented global challenge of Covid-19, I have made it, and so have you. It has been some kind of ride!

Formula One is part of my life and, as illustrated in this book, it has reflected itself in many aspects of the world in which you and I live. We begin our lives born as winners (Born Winners). Growing up, we try to find our own identities to become who we are, through our families, schools and communities (Be Like Kimi). We evolve as individuals, learning new skills in classrooms and the social realm (The Evolution Game). During different phases, we master the mental skills to adapt and overcome adversity when faced with challenges in the unjust world (Shit Happens, Dancing in the Rain & Life is Unfair). As we climb the ladder, we begin to learn the importance of teamwork (Teamwork makes the Dream Work). When our values change over time, we come to terms with conflicting interests at work and/or in social activities (No Friendly Business). We constantly try to find the perfect setup in all aspects of life to achieve and optimise lifestyles (Balancing Act), and acquire essential tools to help and manage relationships (Pick your Battles). Most importantly, we develop perspective and visualise life the way we want it (All About Perspective & The Power of Visualisation). What Formula One drivers are doing on the track is defying the laws of physics, much like how we challenge ourselves against the world.

I hope I have demystified some of the common misconceptions of what Formula One racing is; a physically demanding sport, with power, finesse, mental strength and neck muscles to handle speeds of more than 300kph and forces up to 5G, second only to a fighter jet pilot. Formula One is about going to the edge and finding the limits. It is everything about cooperative effort between human beings and machines, from the factories to the pit garage, to the cockpit. In the meantime, I have tried my best not to give away too many spoilers or uncover too many race outcomes in case you would like to experience watching the races yourself, appreciating through the tightly choreographed spectacle of television. That is to say, I would be thrilled if you become a Formula One fan through reading this book, otherwise I am just as happy that you have finished reading the entire content, leaving the book with or without newly inspired conviction toward life or Formula One racing.

Ayrton Senna, to me, is the greatest Formula One driver, and he once said this, *"On a given day, a given circumstance, you think you have a limit. And you then go for this limit and you touch this limit, and you think, 'Okay, this is the limit'. And so you touch this limit, something happens and you suddenly can go a little bit further. With your mind power, your determination, your instinct, and the experience as well, you can fly very high."*

In retrospective, I never imagined myself becoming a Formula One fan, chasing fast cars year after year. Nor would have I imagined myself becoming an indie writer, chasing words to make sense of the two worlds.

I guess the moral of the story is to never say never, and all things are possible when you start believing it in the first place. Do not let limiting beliefs bind you when you can always go a little bit further. I would encourage you to challenge your limits; if you have dreams, you should chase them as a racing driver would. Opportunities might not present themselves with obvious manifestation, but at times we need to dig deeper to look for the gaps and make the manoeuvre.

> *"If you no longer go for a gap that exists you are no longer a racing driver."*
>
> Ayrton Senna

Formula One is an uncontrollable drama, very much like our life, filled with tons of stuff not always within our grasp; we all have a fair bit of racing ahead in our life. Take these lessons with you and you will be able to steer your car into all the corners and hit the apex, en route to purple sectors, one after another. Keep fine-tuning and adjusting the car setting or the driving style to suit the track and its condition and manage any safety car interventions in your life. Keep your head in the race and remember, the race is not over until you see the chequered flag waving.

Now, live your life to the max and race your heart out.

John Huang

26 June 2020

> *"A lot of people criticise Formula 1 as an unnecessary risk. But what would life be like if we only did what is necessary?"*
>
> Niki Lauda

COOL DOWN LAP

"Grazie!"

Success in Formula One requires a total team effort, as illustrated in this book. Likewise, for the birth of this book, I could not have done it alone.

To my family, my wife and two children, who are the loves of my life, for being the motivation to write. This book is for them. Hoping to conserve the life lessons that will help and cultivate them in their life journeys.

My friends who have supported me in this endeavour, Robert, Peter and Jo. Robert for sharing all our Formula One experiences together. Peter for inspiring me with the idea for this book. Jo for your moral supports in my creative output.

I would like to extend my gratitude to my brother, Johnson. Growing up, he was the alpha male that I looked up to. As much as I was a pest to him, being the younger sibling, I have always admired his abilities and leadership in ways that transform into greater aspiration. It is for this reason, I feel Formula One is an identity that I can genuinely own.

Last but not least, I would like to thank you for reading. For picking up this book, whether it was by chance or for any other reason. I hope it has given you something in return and you have enjoyed my 12 Life Lessons in Formula One.

For that, I say Grazie! Just as Sebastian Vettel says on his radio message to his Ferrari team whenever he wins. Thank you and stay safe.

LESSONS LEARNED

_____

_____

_____

_____

_____

_____

_____

_____

_____

_____

_____

_____

_____

_____